CIVILIZATION AND ITS DISCONTENTS

An Anthropology for the Future?

TWAYNE'S MASTERWORK STUDIES

Robert Lecker, General Editor

CIVILIZATION AND ITS DISCONTENTS

An Anthropology for the Future?

Thomas Parisi

TWAYNE PUBLISHERS
New York

Twayne's Masterwork Studies No. 171

Civilization and Its Discontents: An Anthropology for the Future?
Thomas Parisi

Copyright © 1999 by Twayne Publishers

Twayne Publishers
1633 Broadway
New York, NY 10019

Library of Congress Cataloging-in-Publication Data

Parisi, Thomas.
    Civilization and its discontents : an anthropology for the future?
    / Thomas Parisi.
        p.   cm. — (Twayne's masterwork studies ; no. 171)
    Includes bibliographical references and index.
    ISBN 0-8057-7934-5 (alk. paper)
    1. Freud, Sigmund, 1856–1939. Unbehagen in der Kulture. English.
2. Philosophical anthropology.   3. Ethnopsychology.   I. Title.
II. Series.
BF173.F6823P37   1999
150.19'52—dc21   98-47742
                                                              CIP

This paper meets the requirements of ANSI/NISO Z3948-1992 (Permanence of Paper).

10 9 8 7 6 5 4 3 2 1

Printed in the United States of America

To Marianne, Claire, and Ben,
who have taught me by their example
how interweaving circles of erotic energy,
transformed or otherwise, can make the world anew.

Sketch of Freud by Salvador Dali (1938)
© 1998 Demart Pro Arte,® Geneva/Artists Rights Society (ARS), New York.

Contents

Note on the References and Acknowledgments

With the exception of *Civilization and Its Discontents,* all references to Freud's published works are to *The Standard Edition of the Complete Psychological Works of Sigmund Freud,* translated from the German under the general editorship of James Strachey, in collaboration with Anna Freud, assisted by Alix Strachey and Alan Tyson (London: Hogarth Press and the Institute of Psycho-Analysis, 1953–1974). For *Civilization and Its Discontents,* I have referred to the readily available paperback reprint of what appears in the *Standard Edition,* published by W. W. Norton and Company.

Though writing this little book was largely a solitary event between Freud and me, I was comforted by the confidence that I could count on a great number of other people, and those people did not disappoint me. I hope that in the future I will have occasions to repay their many and substantial kindnesses.

Joyce Block read each chapter in draft form, and then paid for her own coffee at Lula's coffeehouse while we discussed Freud. Joe Incandela read several chapters and in an incredibly neat handwriting posed just the right questions in the margins. Gail Mandell read all but the last two chapters and provided feedback that was, as usual, both insightful and encouraging.

Kevin McDonnell has been a mentor in many different ways over almost two decades; here, he came enthusiastically to my aid in the chapter on ethics and it is much better as a result.

John Shinners offered his expertise as an historian, and I am grateful to him as well as to Tom Bonnell for the support and interest they have shown.

Ann Loux, enthusiastic colleague-editor, had little to do with this specific project, but she has taken an interest in my writing—though we still disagree profoundly about Freud—that has made it, I venture to say, measurably better.

It is not easy these days to be an academic psychologist with a passion for Freud, but my colleagues in the psychology department at Saint Mary's—Joe Miller, Catherine Pittman, Becky Stoddart, and Mary Wood—showed warm if sometimes incredulous interest in the work and offered helpful suggestions that improved the final product.

Several people read individual chapters, shared their views across a range of topics, and helped in many other ways. Thank you Susan Alexander, Joe Bellina, Peg Falls, Tom Fogle, Linda Harrington, Phyllis Kaminski, Renee Kingcaid, Dick Jensen, Beth Newman, Bruno Schlesinger, George Trey, and Doris Watt. Thanks also to Robert Lecker and to all of the people at Twayne and Impressions involved in production. Jennifer Waldburger's careful and perceptive copyediting saved me from several blunders.

Over a decade ago, Saint Mary's College broke with precedent and allowed me to use summer research funds to purchase my personal set of Freud's collected works. See! But seriously, I am thankful to Saint Mary's for the professional home it has become and also more concretely for several summer grants and two sabbatical leaves, the last of which was spent drafting the book. The National Endowment for the Humanities provided funding for several summer projects, including the direction of two summer seminars for high school teachers on Freud. At Saint Mary's, a special thanks to Pat White, and at NEH, to Clay Lewis.

It is impossible to express what is in my heart and soul for the three people to whom I have dedicated the book: my wife, Marianne; our daughter, Claire; and our son, Ben. I think they know that I have enjoyed the solitude I have found working on this project. But the solitude could be enjoyed only because of the knowledge that I was never really alone.

Note on the References and Acknowledgments

Finally, thanks to the many students who have had Freud foisted on them by yours truly, and to my summer seminarians, dedicated and talented high school teachers who came to Indiana in July to read Freud with me. You have challenged me, encouraged me, sometimes frustrated me, and helped me to see more clearly what I wanted to communicate in this study.

Abbreviations

Frequently cited works by Freud are abbreviated as follows:

Comparative Study	"Some points for a comparative study of organic and hysterical paralyses," 1893.
Interpretation	*The Interpretation of Dreams*, 1900.
Three Essays	*Three Essays on the Theory of Sexuality*, 1905.
Five Lectures	*Five Lectures on Psycho-Analysis*, 1909.
TT	*Totem and Taboo*, 1913.
Introductory Lectures	*Introductory Lectures on Psycho-Analysis*, 1916–1917.
Beyond	*Beyond the Pleasure Principle*, 1920.
EI	*The Ego and the Id*, 1923.
AS	*An Autobiographical Study*, 1925.
Consequences	"Some psychical consequences of the anatomical distinction between the sexes," 1925.
Future	*The Future of an Illusion*, 1927.
Civilization	*Civilization and Its Discontents*, 1930.
NIL	*New Introductory Lectures on Psycho-Analysis*, 1933.
Letters	*Letters of Sigmund Freud*, edited by Ernst L. Freud, 1960.

Chronology

Two biographies have been especially helpful in the construction of this chronology: Ronald W. Clark, *Freud: the Man and the Cause* (New York: Random House, 1980), and Peter Gay, *Freud: A Life for Our Time* (New York: Norton, 1988). They are hereafter cited in text.

1856	Sigismund Freud born on May 6 in Freiberg, Moravia, into a household that would itself have been fertile ground for psychoanalytic explorations. Sigismund is the oldest child of Jacob and Amalie (Nathanson) Freud. Jacob has two sons, Emanuel and Philipp, from his first marriage to Sally Kanner. Emanuel is only two years younger than his stepmother, and Philipp is one year older. Emanuel's two oldest children, John and Pauline, are one and two years older, respectively, than their uncle-playmate, Sigismund.
1857–1858	Brother Julius is born but dies in his first year; sister Anna is born. While Freud's mother will refer to her oldest son as "my golden Sigi," she is occupied for much of the first two years of his life with mourning the death of Julius and caring for Anna. Sigismund spends much time with a nursemaid of whom he later retains vivid memories.
1859	The Freud family leaves Freiburg. Jacob, Amalie, Sigismund, and Anna make their way to Vienna; Philipp and Emanuel emigrate to Manchester, England. In England, a country that will always exert a pull on Freud's affections, Charles Darwin's *On the Origin of Species* is published.
1869	Postcards introduced in Austria. Writing to his friend Eduard Silberstein in 1875, Freud curses the invention of postcards: "The world grows more prosaic with every new invention; in the end, letters will fall into disuse and be replaced by telegrams." The theme that every technological advance comes with a human cost will be developed more than 50 years later in *Civilization and Its Discontents*.

1872–1873   Graduates from Gymnasium summa cum laude and prepares for the Matura, required for entrance to the University of Vienna. May 1873: the opening of the World Exhibition; "Black Friday," a series of financial crashes on the Berlin and Vienna stock exchanges that exacerbate anti-Semitism. Begins his studies at the university in the fall of 1873. His original intention is to study law, but he is drawn to science, in part influenced by hearing a poem, "On Nature," attributed to Goethe; registers in the department of medicine.

1874–1875   Adds philosophy to his course of study, signing up with Franz Brentano; the course runs for four consecutive terms. Brentano's major work, *Psychology from an Empirical Standpoint,* which includes substantial discussion of the unconscious and its relation to other realms both physical and mental, is published in 1874. Freud is taken with Brentano, finding him "an ideal man, a believer in God, a teleologist, a Darwinist, and altogether a darned clever fellow."[1]

1875   Summer: travels to England to visit his two brothers in Manchester. Reports in a letter his fondness for Huxley, Darwin, and others on the scientific frontier. Drops "Sigismund" for "Sigmund." Fall: begins zoological studies with Carl Claus. Claus sends Freud to the Zoological Station in Trieste, where he confirms the existence of the testes of the eel.

1877   Begins work in the physiology laboratory of Ernst Brücke, who will become an important mentor. Brücke is dedicated to the proposition that "no forces other than the common physical and chemical ones are active in the organism,"[2] an anti-vitalistic, positivistic, and reductionist approach to science.

1879   Serves a year of compulsory military service, during which he translates into German four essays by John Stuart Mill, a task for which Brentano recommended him. One of the essays deals with the enfranchisement of women, another with Plato; he is impressed with Plato's theory of reminiscence.[3]

1880–1882   Josef Breuer uses the cathartic method with Bertha Pappenheim, who becomes known to the world as "Anna O."

1881   Receives medical degree.

1882   Meets Martha Bernays in April; they become engaged June 17. In July, joins Vienna General Hospital, rotating through internal medicine, psychiatry, and dermatology. He then goes to the department of nervous diseases, where he will stay for three years.

1884   Publishes "On Coca," a report of his experiments using cocaine.

Chronology

1885	In October, arrives in Paris on a four-month traveling fellowship, obtained with Brücke's assistance, to study with the great French neurologist Jean Martin Charcot. Freud comes away from his visit convinced that ideas can create neurological symptoms, a conclusion hard to reconcile with the reductionistic ethos of Brücke's laboratory.
1886	Returns to Vienna in March. Marries Martha in Wandsbek in September. In October, presents his paper on male hysteria to the Imperial Society of Physicians of Vienna. Freud claims not only that hysteria is present in men as well as in women but also that it can be caused by traumatic experience and not constitutional physiological factors alone.
1887	Begins correspondence with Wilhelm Fliess, an ear, nose, and throat specialist and numerologist who will become an intimate confidant. Fliess is the proponent of the "nasal reflex theory of neurosis," which is based on his perception of a similarity between pelvic anatomy and the turbinal bones of the nose. Freud's letters to Fliess will become the most important record of the birth of psychoanalysis, including Freud's self-analysis. Discovered only after Freud's death, they include his "Project for a Scientific Psychology." Mathilde, named after Breuer's wife, is born.[4]
1889	Jean Martin, named after Charcot, is born.
1891	Publishes *On Aphasia*, which offers a functional/dynamic explanation of language disorders, opposing the conventional emphasis on neuroanatomical localization, and thus foreshadows some of the central concepts of psychoanalysis. Oliver, named after Cromwell, is born.
1892	Ernst, named after Brücke, is born.
1893	Sophie, named after a niece of Samuel Hammerschlag, Freud's religion teacher, is born.
1895	With Josef Breuer, publishes *Studies on Hysteria*. Anna, named after a daughter of Samuel Hammerschlag, is born.
1896	Presents "The Aetiology of Hysteria" to the Society of Psychiatry and Neurology, arguing that underlying all hysteria is a scene of actual childhood seduction—the so-called seduction hypothesis. Krafft-Ebing refers to Freud's thesis as a "scientific fairy tale." November: Freud's father dies; Freud begins his self-analysis soon after.
1895–1896	Gustav Mahler at work on his Third Symphony, "which sought to instruct its audience on the importance of dreams and the processes of conscious-unconscious interaction within the human psyche."[5]

1897   September 21: reports to Fliess, "I no longer believe in my *neurotica.*" This move away from the seduction hypothesis paves the way for the Oedipus complex.

1899   *The Interpretation of Dreams* is published late in the year and dated 1900. Arnold Schoenberg composes *Transfigured Night,* signally the "liberation of dissonance" in music.[6] Karl Kraus establishes *Die Fackel.*

1902   Formation of the "Wednesday Society"; founding members, including Alfred Adler and Wilhelm Stekel, meet with Freud on Wednesday evenings in his waiting room. This group later becomes the Vienna Psychoanalytic Society.

1905   Publishes *Jokes and Their Relation to the Unconscious, Three Essays on the Theory of Sexuality,* and "Fragment of an Analysis of a Case of Hysteria," the case of "Dora." Albert Einstein presents the special theory of relativity.

1907   Publishes "Obsessive Actions and Religious Practices." Carl Jung comes to Vienna to meet Freud; according to Jung, they talk nonstop for 13 hours.

1909   Visits America, accompanied by Jung and Sándor Ferenczi, delivering his *Five Lectures* at Clark University and receiving an honorary doctor of law degree. Those attending the lectures include psychologist G. S. Hall, anarchist Emma Goldman, neurologist James Jackson Putnam, and William James, ailing from the heart disease that will kill him within a year. In this, his only visit to America, Freud takes in Coney Island, Niagara Falls, the Adirondack mountains, and his first moving picture, suffering through much of the trip with indigestion.

1910   Jung is elected president of the International Pscho-Analytical Association.

1911   Adler and Stekel defect. Freud worried that, in creating a theory emphasizing the inferiority of psychological and physical characteristics rather than the primacy of sexuality, Adler had "created for himself a world system without love."[7]

1912   Breaks with Jung. In *Transformation and Symbols of the Libido,* Jung took issue with Freud's emphasis on an exclusively sexual libido, arguing instead for a generalized psychological energy.

1912–1913   Publishes *Totem and Taboo.*

1914   Publishes *On the History of the Psycho-Analytic Movement,* beginning with an epigram taken from the coat of arms of the city of Paris: *Fluctuat nec mergitur* ("It is tossed by the waves but it does not sink"). In this polemical history, Freud articulates the differences between his views and those of Jung and

Adler. Publishes "On Narcissism" and, anonymously, "The Moses of Michelangelo." Freud's identification with Moses will continue throughout his life, culminating in *Moses and Monotheism*. On June 28, Archduke Francis Ferdinand, heir to the throne of Austria-Hungary, and his wife, Sophie, are assassinated in Sarajevo while on a goodwill tour of Bosnia. Within a month, Austria-Hungary declares war on Serbia, and most of Europe is drawn into World War I. In *Civilization and Its Discontents*, Freud will speak of the "narcissism of minor differences," an outgrowth of human aggression. Psychoanalysis is used for the treatment of "shell shock." All of Freud's children survive the war; Martin and Ernst serve in the military, while Oliver, an engineer, is employed on construction projects.

1915   Publishes "Thoughts for the Times on War and Death."

1915–1917   The five "papers on metapsychology" are published, Freud's first attempt to present his theory systematically since *The Interpretation of Dreams*. In two successive winter terms, gives a series of lectures at the University of Vienna, published as *Introductory Lectures on Psycho-Analysis*.

1918   November 11: armistice ends World War I.

1919   June 28: the signing of the Treaty of Versailles. Under this and other treaties, the Austro-Hungarian empire is reduced to a fraction of its former size, and enormous reparations are extracted from Germany, paving the way for World War II. To the end of his life, Freud harbors an antipathy toward Woodrow Wilson, whose Fourteen Points and hopes for "peace without victory" are left behind in the peace process.

1920   Daughter Sophie dies suddenly in Hamburg from "the virulent influenza . . . sweeping across an ill-nourished Europe."[8] Publishes *Beyond the Pleasure Principle,* introducing the concept of the death instinct. Maurice Ravel composes *La Valse,* which musically records "the violent death of the nineteenth-century world."[9]

1923   Publishes *The Ego and the Id.* In April, cancer of the mouth and jaw is discovered. Over the next 16 years, Freud will undergo more than 30 operations to remove cancerous tissue, open up passageways, and fit false palates. In *Civilization and Its Discontents*, he will write: "Man . . . has become a kind of prosthetic God. When he puts on all those auxiliary organs he is truly magnificent; but those organs . . . still give him much trouble at times" (42). Nicknames his own prosthesis "the Monster." Sophie's younger son, Heinele, dies of tuberculosis at the age of four. "He was indeed an enchanting little fellow, and I myself was aware of never having loved a human being, certainly never a child, so much," Freud writes.[10]

1924   The Hogarth Press, founded by Leonard and Virginia Woolf, begins publishing Freud's work.

1925   Publishes *An Autobiographical Study.*

1926   Publishes *Inhibitions, Symptoms, and Anxiety* and *The Question of Lay Analysis.*

1927   Publishes *The Future of an Illusion.*

1929   The start of the Great Depression.

1930   Publishes *Civilization and Its Discontents.*

1933   Publication of *Why War?,* an exchange of letters between Freud and Einstein. In Germany, Hitler appointed chancellor. May 10: 5,000 swastika-bearing students take part in a burning of books, including the works of Freud and Einstein, in Berlin.

1937   Publishes "Analysis Terminable and Interminable."

1938   Hitler enters Austria. On June 3, a reluctant Freud leaves Vienna for Paris, and then goes on to London. Under pressure, Freud signs a document stating that he has been properly treated by the Gestapo. Four of Freud's sisters will perish in the concentration camps.

1939   *Moses and Monotheism* published in Holland. In the spring of the year, the New York World's Fair opens with a mood of "acute hope."[11] September 1: Hitler invades Poland. September 22: aided by his physician Max Schur, Freud lapses into a coma and dies the next morning.

LITERARY AND
HISTORICAL CONTEXT

In the new home (1938)
The Freud Museum.

1

Historical and Intellectual Context

Freud was at the intersection of many streams of influence. On the one hand, there are those currents that have to do relatively specifically with the scientific and philosophical questions that led to the development of the Freudian enterprise. On the other, there is the fertile artistic, literary, and political culture that constituted fin de siècle Vienna. I will discuss these broader influences first, turning later in the chapter to those more specifically connected to Freud's enterprise.

Freud and Vienna are inextricably intertwined. When, at the age of three or four, he settled with his family into a gritty mercantile area of the city, the emperor, Franz Joseph, had only recently decreed the beginning of a massive urban-redevelopment project that would replace the city's old fortress walls with the grandeur of the Ringstrasse. Freud's long life unfolded within this crucible of modernity. Although he would travel to Italy, to Paris, to Greece, to Berlin, in his adolescence to England, and once to America, his home was Vienna. He left the city for good only reluctantly in the spring of 1938, at age 82, just weeks after Hitler had annexed Austria, and even then with a feeling that he was "like a soldier deserting his post" (Clark, 507).

A central claim in *Civilization and Its Discontents* is that life is a never-ending struggle between the constructive forces of Eros and the destructive forces of the death instinct. It would be wrong to suggest that Freud's conclusions within his theory building were simply the reflections of the culture in which he was embedded. And yet one of the first things that one realizes in studying Vienna at the end of the nineteenth century is that it was a culture simultaneously in the throes of a long, slow death and a scintillating, feverish birth.

In civic and political terms, it was the process of decay that was most evident. By the 1860s, the power and grandeur of the old Habsburg empire were in eclipse. Defeat in the war with Prussia had ended Austria-Hungary's hopes for "hegemony in the German-speaking world,"[1] and the rest of the century witnessed a series of hostilities among the Balkan nations, hostilities that are suddenly sadly familiar at the end of the twentieth century. The culmination of all of these "small" wars was the assassination of the archduke Francis Ferdinand in Sarajevo, unleashing World War I.

Vienna, the center of the dying empire, had become, in the words of Karl Kraus, "the proving ground for world destruction" (Janik and Toulmin, 67). The construction of the Ringstrasse was symbolic of the attempt to pull the Habsburg monarchy out of its medieval modus operandi, and at the same time it represented the very end of such monarchical forms of government, the triumph of constitutionalism and popular sovereignty over the divine right of the emperor and "of secular culture over religious faith."[2] Freud as well as other citizens hoped that these moves toward political liberalism would lessen the anti-Semitism that was, not surprisingly, endemic in the capital city of the Habsburg (i.e., the Holy Roman) empire. And for a while these hopes were realized. But by the 1890s, with the election of Karl Leuger as mayor of Vienna, anti-Semitism reached new heights, and the more general failures of reform were made clear by the emergence of mass political movements.[3]

But as the empire crumbled, modern varieties of consciousness were born. To what extent were literature, the arts, philosophy, and the sciences affected by all of these political upheavals and dislocations? In a word, enormously: "[T]he central weaknesses manifested in the decline and fall of the Habsburg Empire struck deep into the lives and experiences of its citizens, shaping and conditioning the . . . preoccupations of artists and writers in all fields of thought and culture, even the most abstract" (Janik and Toulmin, 14). In the view of historian Carl Schorske, the cultural flowering of Vienna at the end of the nineteenth century reflected disenchantment in the face of the failures of political liberalism and was a product of a turning inward, of a preoccupation with the possibilities of the exploration of the self. This cultural flowering is reflected in dramatic developments in art, architecture, literature, and music as well as in science and philosophy. We can get no more than a hint of this flowering here, but we will note that in many specific instances there are parallels to Freud's work in the emerging enterprise of psychoanalysis, which is also concerned, of course, with the possibilities of the exploration of the self.

As one example, we can note interesting parallels between the birthing of psychoanalysis and developments in music. It is unlikely that Freud followed these developments himself, his relationship to music being "rather distant and quizzical"; he enjoyed some operas, but his tastes were far from avant garde (Gay 1988, 168). While he interrupted a vacation in 1910 to see Gustav Mahler as a client "because 'he could not refuse a man of Mahler's worth,' "[4] it is unlikely that he heard much, if any, of the pathbreaking music Mahler and Schoenberg were composing at the time. Nevertheless, it is interesting to note that at the same time Freud was making some of his seminal explorations, Mahler, in his Second Symphony (*Resurrection*), was asking about the nature of suffering,[5] also a central question in Freud's speculations in *Civilization and Its Discontents*. In his Third Symphony, Mahler "sought to instruct [his] audience on the importance of dreams and the processes of conscious-unconscious interactions within the human psyche" (McGrath, 80). And in his last, unfinished symphony he would dramatically mark the "death of tonality,"[6] leaving it for Schoenberg to break through to a new harmonic system.

Freud was more attuned to literary and scientific-philosophical developments. For example, he told the playwright Arthur Schnitzler "that he had long been aware of a far reaching correspondence between their views on psychological and erotic problems" and referred to Schnitzler as his doppelgänger.[7] And like many thinkers of his day, he was very much influenced by Ernst Mach, an implication of whose work in physics, philosophy, and the emerging field of experimental psychology is that the self "is not a substantial entity but a complex of sensory perceptions.... Just as Mach denied the existence of a uniform ... inner world ... Freud [would] split the soul into segments" (Spiel, 134).

In different ways over the course of Freud's long life, political issues played a significant role in his development. From autobiographical material in *The Interpretation of Dreams,*[8] we know that his first career aspirations were to law and government service. During the 1860s and 1870s, when the hopes for political liberalism in Vienna were at their highest, these ambitions of a young Jewish boy were not totally unrealistic. And even as Freud turned away from these aspirations for a legal career and toward science, medicine, and the founding of psychoanalysis, political themes continued to be reflected in his work. For example, he was fond of using political analogies to describe the workings of the "psychic apparatus," and some of his most humorous examples of "parapraxes"—slips or mistakes that reveal unconscious motive—are taken from accounts of political events reported in the Viennese newspapers of the day. More significantly, the cataclysms of the Great War and its aftermath— which continued through the beginning of World War II—had a significant influence on his work and his worldview (although it is incorrect to say that he argued straight from geopolitics to the idea of a death instinct; Freud insisted, and the evidence bears him out, that he came to the death instinct mostly through clinical phenomena [Gay 1988]).

One of the hallmarks of fin de siècle Vienna is that more than in other places and in other eras, everything seemed to be connected to everything else. From a distance, there is certainly validity to the argument that the political, intellectual, and artistic climates were interdependent, that in a real sense this cultural flowering could have occurred only in that time and place and given only those particular historical contingencies.

However, it is also true that for each particular development one could trace a number of influences that were less directly connected to the wider cultural milieu. And this is more true of the development of Freud's work than of those in the arts and literature. Although we cannot, especially in the case of fin de siècle Vienna, minimize the role of wider cultural influences, it is also true to a significant degree that "the Vienna that Freud constructed for himself was not the Vienna of the court, the café, the salon, or the operetta" (Gay 1988, 10). This is in part because Freud was, throughout his student and professional life, remarkably disciplined and focused. Certainly the depth of his immersion in classical literature is an important element in understanding the development of his insights; to take a simple example, his concept of the Oedipus complex obviously depends on a more than passing familiarity with Greek tragedy and with Shakespeare. But it is also true that the Vienna Freud "constructed for himself" was very much concerned with a specific set of scientific and philosophical issues that are not readily conjured up when one thinks of fin de siècle Vienna. It is to these that I now turn.

By the time Freud left the Gymnasium and entered the University of Vienna, he had decided on a career in medicine. In an autobiographical statement written in 1925, he tells us that there were two reasons for his decision. The first was his interest in Darwinian theory, which held out the hope "of an extraordinary advance in our understanding of the world."[9] The second was hearing a poem attributed to Goethe, "On Nature," "an emotional ... hymn celebrating an eroticized Nature" (Gay 1988, 24). The running together of these two currents, one soberly empirical, the other romantic and metaphysical, set the stage for a pattern in Freud's intellectual life. Indeed, the essence of *Civilization and Its Discontents* is the application of what are empirical facts, in Freud's view anyway, to metaphysical questions of life and death.

In this connection, the influence of Franz Brentano was significant. During his years at university, Freud took four of Brentano's courses. Brentano was then writing the work for which he is best known, *Psychology from the Empirical Standpoint*, which explores, among other subjects, dynamic interactions between conscious and unconscious elements of the mind.

But although Brentano's treatment of this topic no doubt had an impact on Freud, a running conversation between the two was even more influential. Brentano's philosophical positions challenged Freud, who was already committed to a naturalistic view of the world. Brentano was an empiricist; he believed that our conclusions about the world and the mind should be based firmly on experience and scientific evidence. However, he was also a theist and therefore had little commitment to the worldview materialism offered. Freud was stumped by Brentano's positions and by his forceful and persuasive exposition: "He demonstrates the existence of God with as little bias and as much precision as another might argue the advantage of the wave over the emission theory." Freud's encounter with Brentano presages his preoccupation with the question of science as Weltan-schauung. Although the Freud of *Civilization and Its Discontents* seems to have settled comfortably into a world without God, his encounter with Brentano was formative, at the time forcing him to say that "[f]or the time being, I have ceased to be a materialist and am not yet a theist."[10]

Brentano's influence is important because it forced Freud to question his most basic assumptions—about the world, and about the place of human beings in that world. Something similar happened in his encounters with his two most important mentors, Ernst Brücke and Jean Charcot. The precipitate of these relationships was the birth of psychoanalysis.

Freud began work in Brücke's laboratory of physiology in 1877, and over the next several years he completed some elegant work in the histology of the nervous system. In the 1840s, Brücke was part of a group of physiologists, the Berlin School, who were committed to combating a romantic and vitalistic biology, precisely the variety of thinking about biology that inspired the poem on nature that so influenced Freud. Together, these physiologists

> pledged a solemn oath to put into power this truth: no other forces than the common physical-chemical ones are active within the organism. In those cases which cannot at the time be explained by these forces one has either to find the specific way or form of their action by means of the physical-mathematical method, or to assume new forces equal in dignity to the chemical-

physical forces inherent in matter, reducible to the force of attraction and repulsion.[11]

That the young Freud, now a medical student, worked quite happily in Brücke's laboratory may seem remarkable given that the enterprise of psychoanalysis, still in the future, would attribute causal status to forces quite different from the "common physical-chemical ones." It is impossible, however, to understand the development of psychoanalysis without considering this early influence. Throughout his life, Freud would argue that psychoanalysis was part of the scientific Weltanschauung. In part, this view reflected his hope that all of the phenomena he had unearthed would indeed be reducible to the kinds of causes listed in the oath. As well, Freud insisted that these phenomena belonged to the natural world, and in the development of this claim one sees the deep influence of Darwin and of evolutionary ideas in general. Thus the strain of reductionism and positivism seen in the oath taken by Brücke and his colleagues was very influential in the formative years of Freud's professional development.

In 1885, with the aid of Brücke's decisive letter of recommendation, Freud received a traveling fellowship that took him to Paris to study with the great neurologist Jean Martin Charcot. At the Salpêtrière clinic, Charcot was demonstrating that hysterical symptoms, in men as well as in women, could be treated using hypnosis, and further that hysterical symptoms could be created by suggestion while the subject was in a hypnotic trance. These demonstrations were crucial to the development of Freud's discoveries. They constituted a reversal of the causal stream as it is usually conceived and certainly as it was conceived by anyone shaped in the intellectual ambience of Brücke's laboratory: physical events lead to mental events. What Freud learned in Charcot's clinic is that ideas can cause symptoms—that mental events can cause physical events—which is a cornerstone of psychoanalysis.[12]

Freud also came away from his experience with Charcot predisposed to believing that sexual matters played a formative role in hysteria and neurosis. In his essay on the history of the psychoanalytic movement, Freud recalls Charcot's emphasis on the sexual conflict that he saw at the base of these disorders: "[I]n this sort of case, it's always a question of the genitals—always, always, always."[13] On his return to Vienna in the spring of 1886, Freud continued his relationship with Josef Breuer, whom he had met in Brücke's laboratory. Breuer was also convinced, on the basis of work with such patients as the famous Anna O., described in Breuer and Freud's collaborative work, *Studies in Hysteria* (1895), that sexual content lay at the base of neurosis.

It is within this historical context that Freud created the foundational works of psychoanalysis, *The Interpretation of Dreams* (1900) and *Three Essays on the Theory of Sexuality* (1905). The focus of the first, a masterpiece of literature and autobiography as well as of science (its most controversial dimension), is the first pillar of psychoanalysis: the dynamic unconscious, the claim that the most important determinants of our actions occur without our awareness but nevertheless reflect our personal histories. *Three Essays,* in turn, develops the second pillar: that the contents of this unconscious motor of psychic life have always to do with sexuality.

In both works, one sees the influence of Freud's immersion in the life of the laboratory à la Brücke: the attempt to anchor conjectures about the psyche to what he knows to be true about the brain, the attempt to keep the mind firmly within the biological realm. But both works also show the influence of Freud's clinical experience, which included not only his work with Charcot and his own hysterical patients back in Vienna but also his self-analysis. What Freud saw out of these vectors of his experience was that the human psyche is subject to a variety of the "common" forces of attraction and repulsion that Brücke and the Berlin group referred to but that these forces are not subject to the usual physicochemical laws because the psyche is, in the broadest possible sense, a biological organism moving through history, a history about which it can never fully be sentient.

Freud lived a long life, and the historical context for his work, and for understanding the view of life presented in *Civilization and Its Discontents,* of course continues beyond 1905 to encompass the continuing demise of the Habsburg empire; the ravages of the Great War, which forever destroyed the world that existed before it; the economic consequences of the war for Germany and Austria, which would persist well into the 1920s; the Great Depression; and finally, the rise of Nazism and the annexation of Austria.

His theory would continue to evolve within this broader context. From a relatively simple model of unconscious, dynamic psychic conflict would come the mature model of id, ego, and super-ego; from the first postulation of infantile sexuality would come ideas about the role of narcissism and self-love and the claim that conscience grows from loss and guilt; from the postulation of a pleasure principle, the apparently bizarre idea of a death instinct would emerge.

But without minimizing the significant modifications in Freud's theory that took place from 1905 until his death in London in 1939, it can still be said that the early years were foundational. This is not surprising, if indeed we live in the world that Freud discovered, one in which the "future, which the dreamer pictures as the present, has been moulded by his indestructible wish into a perfect likeness of the past" (*Interpretation*, 660).

2

The Importance of
Civilization and Its Discontents

"Life, as we find it, is too hard for us," Freud says in *Civilization* (23). Although he is speaking from within the framework of his psychoanalytic explorations, this is also something he learned from personal experience. For several years he had been coping with the constant pain of the jaw cancer that would eventually claim his life; from 1923 on, he would undergo more than 30 operations, leaving his mouth and jaw mostly prosthetic by the end. In 1920 he lost his beloved daughter Sophie to an influenza epidemic that was sweeping across Europe, and only a few weeks after the first detection of his cancer, Freud's grandson Heinele—Sophie's son—died of tuberculosis at the age of four, a loss that hit Freud particularly hard.

Beyond these personal tribulations, Freud in 1929 could feel both the devastation of the Great War and the consequences of the peace, consequences that were already setting the stage for the next conflagration. When Freud left Vienna in 1938, he was only too aware of the evils that were about to overwhelm Europe and could only mourn for his four sisters who would perish in the concentration camps.

But although written against the backdrop of these events, *Civilization* draws its power from Freud's claim that a fundamental discontent, an existential unease, is not contingent on historical particulars but rather is a necessary outgrowth of a deeply historical and, in the broadest sense, biological legacy; our unease and our humanity are inextricably intertwined, our wishes for peace and happiness therefore "at loggerheads with the whole world, with the macrocosm as much as with the microcosm" (25). Freud believed that exploring these depths could, in addition to providing an understanding of how our moral precepts emerged, also point the way toward the good—the ethical—life. Thus we must "get to know the much trampled soil from which our virtues proudly spring" (*Interpretation*, 659) to understand why it is "that people ... underestimate what is of true value in life" (*Civilization*, 10).

Civilization is in part, then, an essay on ethics that develops its arguments through a summing up of Freud's empirical work and his conclusions about the ways of the natural world, of which human beings are thoroughly a part. In composing it, Freud recapitulated all of his theoretical formulations. The central theme of the work—that happiness is an impossibility in civilized life and renunciation of desire a necessity—depends on the basic Freudian formulations of an instinctual id following the pleasure principle and of a dynamic, conflictual unconscious. That we are seekers after satisfaction means that we are sexual creatures. That we renounce our wishes for immediate gratification means only that we are guilty creatures—because of our common Oedipal history—and it is only out of that guilt that whatever morality we have surfaces. Further, out of this renunciation comes all of the products of civilization, due to the "eternal battle" of Eros and Thanatos, a duality—and Freud was forever fond of dualities—that returns us to his first formulation of pleasure as the reduction of tension. Death, in the Freudian sense, is a return to the tensionless state that preceded the development of both the individual and culture. Finally, Freud implores us to put our energies into work and love, in the hope that Eros will win the day "in the struggle with his equally immortal adversary" (112).

It is difficult to discuss the importance of any one of Freud's works without also considering the larger body of claims that flow from his life work. This larger question—does *Freud* matter?—will tacitly be with us for this entire study. But there are a few things to be said immediately.

First, let us acknowledge that Freud, like many intellectual giants, was in several respects deeply flawed. As we shall see, some have argued that Freud the man was so corrupt that we should disregard his claims altogether, and these voices have become increasingly shrill over the past two decades. The extent to which this human frailty does or should deflect us from a consideration of his worldview will be considered more fully in the next chapter as well as in chapter 9.

Second, distaste, even disgust, is a common response when first entering the world Freud describes in his writings. We don't like the Freudian world because it appears dark, driven by instincts aggressive and sexual, hopelessly conflicted, doomed ultimately to destruction. We shall see that this view of the Freudian world is incomplete, inadequate, oversimplified, and in important ways, simply wrong.

Finally, though, however much his reputation has suffered, and however repugnant we find his claims, Freud "is inescapable."[1] Whether we warm to his central claims or are repelled by them, we often define ourselves in Freudian terms: that we are creatures in conflict; that much of what we achieve is based on renunciation; that our movements toward objects of desire in the present have much to do with our relationships with objects of desire in the past. In short, we describe the world to ourselves in a Freudian way even as we deny the validity of the world Freud described.

3

Critical Reception:
The Abuses and Uses of Freudianism

to us he is no more a person
now but a whole climate of opinion
—W. H. Auden, "In Memory of Sigmund Freud"

In an essay written for Freud's 80th birthday, Thomas Mann wrote optimistically about the prospects for Freud's legacy. "This physicianly psychologist will ... be honored as the path-finder toward a humanism of the future" he said, and found in Freud the foundation "of a new anthropology ... which shall be the future dwelling of a wiser and freer humanity."[1] From the vantage point of these last years of the twentieth century, with Freud, the man and the work, under heavy attack, this remark may seem both quaint and naive. I will take a closer look at this newest wave of criticism at the end of this chapter and more fully explore the implications of Mann's assessment in chapter 9. To begin, though, it can be said simply and accurately enough that Freud's body of work—with *Civilization and Its Discontents* serving as its distillation—is today in the paradoxical position of being at once the most reviled and most influential in modern intellectual history.

Because Freud believed that he was offering a scientific understanding of the human predicament, it is in some sense only reasonable to expect that criticism would threaten to overshadow the work. After all, it is the nature of science to attempt to refute hypotheses and conjectures about the question under study.[2] But the scrutiny that Freud's theory has always received indicates that something more is at stake than a simple and straightforward scientific claim. Aside from the newest wave of attack, there are three long-standing bases for the controversies that surround Freud: the claims themselves, the nature of Freud's method, and the institutional culture of psychoanalysis.

THE CLAIMS

Never guilty of false modesty, it was Freud himself who described psychoanalysis as delivering the "third and most wounding blow" to our self-conceptions (*Introductory Lectures*, 285). Copernicus displaced us from the center of the universe. Darwin displaced us from our special position apart from the rest of the animal kingdom. Freud told us not only that we must consider ourselves more like the other animals than we had previously, for like them we are driven by instinctual urges, but also that the capacity that seems to identify us in the tree of life— our capacity for reason—has little to do with our central motivations. In the Freudian scheme, although we must depend on reason in some sense as our one hope, it has at best a fragile hold on the passions.

THE NATURE OF FREUD'S METHOD

Freud always insisted that psychoanalysis was part of the "scientific Weltanschauung." He believed that "the intellect and the mind are objects for scientific research in exactly the same way as any non-human things" and that his own explorations followed the canons of science—"the intellectual working-over of carefully scrutinized observations."³ Freud's view of what constitutes scientific activity is narrow and can sound defensive, ignoring the role that intuition and imagination have played in great scientific discoveries and even, though perhaps to a lesser degree, in routine scientific work. This is ironic, since Freud's enterprise, however one finally judges it as science, is unquestionably a rich mix of imagination and intuition as well as observation, induction, and deduction.

Many in the social sciences have criticized Freud because his claims have not, in their specifics, been supported by laboratory experiments and because the phenomena he described—repression, for example, or the Oedipus complex, or the latent content of dreams—are difficult if not impossible to replicate in well-controlled studies.⁴ But contexts for the search for knowledge, even those that we agree are scientific, differ substantially, and replication within controlled laboratory conditions is not a sine qua non of science in general. Many of the things we believe, on the basis of sound and uncontroversial scientific work, were not discovered in a laboratory setting, nor could they have been. Evolutionary theory and cosmology, two examples, both rely on naturalistic observation rather than on the manipulation and control of variables in an experimental setting.⁵

But even keeping in mind a very broad definition of science—we can take Freud's: the intellectual working-over of carefully scrutinized observations—there are problems with construing psychoanalysis as simply science. Probably the most damning observation about psychoanalysis and its claim to be scientific in the usual sense is that its concepts can and have been used to explain opposite observations, for example when the existence of an aggressive drive is said to have been supported by either the presence or absence of violent behavior (Fisher and Greenberg, 1977). Freud's method is problematic, then, even when evaluated by the broadest and most general standards of science. Freud's work is different even from that in the sciences just mentioned—evolutionary biology and cosmology—which cannot rely exclusively or even primarily on manipulation and control of experimental variables.

Jonathan Lear, a philosopher who has turned his perceptive eye to the psychoanalytic enterprise, has argued, however, that the difficulty in encompassing Freud's method within the canons of science as usually construed reveals something important not only about both psychoanalysis and the sciences but also about what it means to be human. Because psychoanalysis is a science of human subjectivity, it can never hew to the kind of observational neutrality that is the goal of "the uncontestably empirical sciences." Furthermore,

> if one takes the idea of [a science of subjectivity] to heart, one cannot just start with the category of science and ask whether psychoanalysis fits into it; [instead,] the very category of science must be reevaluated. Freud's contribution is not so much to add a new offspring to the existing family of sciences as to encourage us to rethink the basis of kinship.... Rarely in life is one given the opportunity to become conscious of an assumption by which one's own culture lives. But in this debate—"It is not a science"/ "Yes it is"—one can start to see an obsessional strategy being played out at the cultural level. What assumption does this debate hide and protect? That the world itself is devoid of value, purpose, or meaning.[6]

In his own way, Lear is raising the question Thomas Mann articulated: what is the anthropology implicit in the Freudian corpus, and how does it differ from one that flows from attempts to construe the human being by relying solely on "uncontestably empirical" methods?

THE INSTITUTIONAL CULTURE OF PSYCHOANALYSIS

Finally, in addition to Freud's claims and the methods he employed, the institutional culture in which psychoanalysis matured adds to the controversy. For a number of reasons, foremost among them perhaps Freud's failure to secure an academic title or position until relatively late in life, psychoanalytic theory developed within insular groups isolated from the broader stream of academic or intellectual discourse that, it is rightly argued, would have allowed it to respond more flexibly to the kind of criticism that fosters productive change.[7] Because of this history, the claims of Freud and his followers can seem hollow and dogmatic, based more on authority than on reasoned argument.

Critical Reception: The Abuses and Uses of Freudianism

In his review of *Civilization and Its Discontents,* John Strachey wrote,

> It is of no little interest that [Freud's view] concurs so well with the view of humanity expressed with perfect unanimity by the poets. It is moving that this, the first man who has found a method—as yet, of course, crude and imperfect, but even so the *first* method—scientifically to investigate the human psyche should have discovered there almost exactly what the poets have found by intuition.[8]

One possible implication, of course, is that Freud was correct in the worldview he constructed over his long career—a tragic view of life that is fully realized in the compact essay under study here—and that this is why we find his conclusions so disturbing. It is interesting to remember that the two other figures in Freud's pantheon—Copernicus and Darwin—are today universally acknowledged as having been correct in their claims about the nature of the world and our place in it despite the great upheaval those claims created.

Strachey's was a "glowing review ... suffused with respectful admiration" for Freud in general and *Civilization* in particular (Keill, 592). This was not typical, however; the reviews of the book ranged widely, in total exhibiting a variety not different from the range of reactions to Freud we find today. Catlin, while characterizing the book as "the authentic handiwork of a master," went on to criticize it for not sufficiently developing its arguments, in particular about the "mystic entities" Eros and the death instinct (in Keill, 596–97). R. L. Duffus argued that "it is too late ... to discuss Freud because he takes certain of his own theories with an oracular solemnity." Still, Duffus showed a sensitivity to the large task Freud had set himself in his life work even as he criticized it: "[U]ntil the human consciousness, not to mention the subconsciousness, can be dissected as accurately as the human liver there will be gaps in the Freudian chain of proof. Considering this little volume apart from any others of the Freudian collection one is frequently aware of those gaps" (in Keill, 598–600). In that last sentence, Duffus anticipated one of my goals in *this* volume, namely to enrich our sense of Freud's philosophical view by exploring its connections to his other work.

"It seems the irony of fate that one with so joyous a name as Freud should be the founder of so unjoyous a dispensation, and an apostle of despair," wrote Joseph Jastrow. But Jastrow, a prominent psychologist of his day, appreciated the complexity of Freud's views: "How convincing all this may be, it is not easy to determine; there is so much more to be said and by such diverse voices." His review also addressed an issue that is still with us, namely the extent to which Freud's personal issues may have overlapped his professional agenda: "The mood of despondency [in the book] may be an aftermath of the disruptive war, yet not a personal reaction, for in that convulsive struggle Freud kept his head and his heart, yet added the death instinct to the category of momentous urges" (in Keill, 601–03).

As I mentioned in the previous chapter, it is difficult to separate the ideas and claims in *Civilization* from the rest of Freud's work. While the appearance of a specific work of course prompted reviews, many of those reviews were similar in content to topical essays that aimed at getting a more inclusive sense of the implications of Freudianism. The authors of these topical essays, as a group, can be characterized as sympathetic to the Freudian worldview and as often having an accurate and deep understanding of Freud's theory, even if their hopes for what Freudian therapy could achieve sometimes seem wildly overblown. Walter Lippman, writing in the *New Republic* in 1915, argued that Freud meets with such controversy precisely because "we are ourselves the subject matter of his science, and in a most intimate and drastic way." Lippman, like Freud, believed that an intellectual revolution comparable to the one Darwin initiated was in the works: "In Freud I believe we have a man of much the same quality.... He has set up a reverberation in human thought and conduct of which few as yet dare to predict the consequences."[9] And Clement Wood, writing in the *New York Times Book Review,* believed that Freud's enterprise "is a matter that no thinking man or woman can ignore ... except on peril of missing the present's finest key to the riddles whose first answers may be gained by man, but whose final solutions will always remain locked in the untelic and uncognitive energy that brought them to birth" (in Keill, 435). In his choice of the words *untelic* and *uncognitive,* Wood picked up on two essential dimensions of Freud's view of human life: its thorough embeddedness in a radically Darwinian world devoid of purpose and its core irrationality. But his insight was matched by what we today recognize as a real naivete about the possibilities inherent in psychotherapy of any kind. Acknowledging that "psychoanalysis is out of reach financially for the average man or woman," he recommended it anyway "as a way out for all, and the only way out for many," because "until the inner life is individuated and set in order, man's effectiveness is curtailed and blocked in a thousand unguessed ways" (in Keill, 437).

It is still an open question whether the view Freud propounded in *Civilization* and other works is indeed a way to a wiser or freer humanity, but the evolving importance of Freud's work is seen in the multitude of responses to the question posed implicitly by Thomas Mann.

Uncountable critics have used psychoanalytic concepts to explore the creation and form of literature as well as the reader's response to it. This activity ranges from the analysis of a single work to entire theories of what literature is.[10] Similarly, a large assortment of works ranging across the fields of literary criticism, philosophy, and sociology begin with basic Freudian premises and explore their implications for living and being. Examples of this work include *Eros and Civilization* by Herbert Marcuse and *Life against Death* by Norman O. Brown. More recently, Paul Ricouer's *Freud and Philosophy* explores the relationship between Freud's method and what he calls a "hermeneutics of suspicion." And the response to Freud's claims from the feminist community, which have been important for many fields of endeavor, will be explored more fully in chapter 8. Examples of this work include de Beauvoir's *Second Sex,* probably the pathbreaker in the feminist response to Freud, Kate Millett's *Sexual Politics,* and Juliet Mitchell's *Psychoanalysis and Feminism.*

That Freud's work might be the source of an entire anthropology, however, is even more powerfully evident in literary fiction. Canonical works such as *Hamlet* and *Macbeth* are just two examples, which of course preceded Freud's work by hundreds of years. Then there is the literature of our own time, which like many of Shakespeare's plays also supports the validity of a Freudian view without intending to do so. The writing of Virginia Woolf leaps to mind. Both the formal structure of such novels as *To the Lighthouse* and *Mrs. Dalloway* and the stories they tell come remarkably close to the "primary process" of a Freudian dynamic unconscious. Furthermore, the tragic themes in both novels and in Woolf's personal life seem not very distant from the ones explored in *Civilization*. Similarly, James Joyce's explorations, in *Dubliners* and *Ulysses,* of the primacy of sexual motivation and multiple streams of consciousness parallel central Freudian themes.

For none of these examples do I mean to suggest that the themes of the works can or should be neatly reduced to simple Freudian formulations. My point, rather, is that the themes they develop and the techniques they employ speak to the validity of the Freudian anthropology. And this is the case whether or not the authors owe any intellectual debt to Freud. For example, what Virginia Woolf read of Freud she did not much like, even though it was her Hogarth Press that first published Freud in English. And although D. H. Lawrence eventually became much enamored of Freud's ideas about sexuality,[11] he wrote *Sons and Lovers,* which is filled with what we now call Oedipal themes, before "he had any direct or detailed acquaintance with [Freud's work], a fact which might be taken as striking independent confirmation of Freud's doctrine" (Eagleton, 174). More recently, John Irving, in such novels as *The World According to Garp* and *The Cider House Rules,* has seemed passionately interested in a kind of eternal battle between Eros and death, a theme he amusingly and perceptively labels the "under toad."

The continuing and manifold response to Freud in the humanities reinforces the claim I put forward in discussing Strachey's review of *Civilization:* the convergence of both scientific and poetic explorations of reality suggests the likelihood of some deep truth in Freud's claims. But in the last years of this century, the possibility of a Freudian anthropology has come under virulent attack from the communities of biological psychiatry and the neurosciences as well as from scholars in the history and philosophy of science.[12] This recent response, different from the one I described earlier in the chapter, which focused relatively dispassionately on scientific problems in Freud's theory, has two main elements.

First, some of these critics are concerned that what they take to be error and fraud in the development of Freud's claims are directly and significantly responsible for social ills that face us today. For example, Jeffrey Masson achieved fame (or infamy, depending on one's point of view) in the 1980s arguing that Freud's move away from the "seduction hypothesis" was made only for crass personal and political reasons and that Freud's final legacy is a cultural history of hidden child abuse.[13]

Second, critics in biological psychiatry, neuroscience, and the history and philosophy of science seek to replace the Freudian anthropology with one that is firmly anchored in a reductionistic biology. Their basic claim is that what we know about the brain is sufficient to reject Freud's claims about the significance of the interplay of unconscious dynamics, instinctual drives, and early experience in understanding who we are. In this view, however Freud's claims were arrived at, they should be rejected because they are, in the light of modern science, simply wrong: a truer and more useful anthropology, a more freeing one, to invoke Mann once again, will be based firmly in biology and in the neurosciences in particular.[14]

What these two views share is a critique of Freud motivated, in different ways, by a desire to further their own particular agendas. In the first case, things become ironic. Masson, for example, would rid the world of abusive behavior toward children, a laudable aim to be sure, but his use of Freud to forward his own politics (a politics Freud would have agreed with, by and large) is completely exploitative. In another context, the debate over "recovered memory syndrome," Freud has been blamed both for the idea that memories may have been "made up" and the claim that they may be repressed.

I will return to these issues in the last chapter, but it should be said now that it is wrong to depict the current debate as being between devilish, politically motivated reductionists and angelic psychoanalysts. The case is more complex and perhaps can best be encapsulated by an event that is unfolding as I write. In 1995, the Library of Congress planned to mount an exhibit on Freud's legacy. But soon after word got out, a group of scientists, philosophers, and other academics mounted a protest of the planned exhibit. Their claim—and they are correct here—is that the advisory board for the exhibit was too uncritical of Freud, consisting of many analysts and including the director of the Freud Archives, an institution that is largely responsible for the continuing insularity of the psychoanalytic community. In short, the protesters were concerned that the exhibit would present a picture of Freud that was inappropriately uncritical and positive. However, as we have seen here, many of the people who mounted this protest have also been uncritical in their attacks on Freud.

For now, the plans for exhibit have been shelved—and to paraphrase the last sentence of *Civilization,* it is hard to know what the final outcome will be.[15] What is clear, despite a recent newsweekly cover story that asked, "Is Freud dead?"[16] is that the anthropology that Freud offered over a long and fruitful life, and that is encapsulated in the essay to which we now turn, continues to be the object of an unsurpassed and rich response.

A READING

4

The Instincts

The theory of the instincts is psychoanalysis in its most opaque and most unsympathetic form.
—Norman O. Brown, *Life against Death*

In *Beyond the Pleasure Principle*, Freud refers to the instincts as "at once the most important and the most obscure element of psychological research."[1] His ideas about the instincts were always changing, and there is no one place in Freud's body of work where one can find a straightforward theory about them. Nevertheless, his final conception, on which the worldview described in *Civilization* depends, is admirable for its simplicity and symmetry, even as it remains controversial.

My aim in this chapter is to elucidate the concepts of the sex instinct and the death instinct as Freud understood them. This is a necessary first step in a reading of *Civilization* for two reasons. First, what Freud meant by sex and death is radically different from our everyday notions of the terms. Sex, for Freud, ultimately has less to do with the mechanics of reproduction—"the old in-out," as Anthony Burgess put it—and more with a kind of existential seeking of a satisfaction that proves ever elusive; it is an attempt to recapture or return to a lost peaceful state. Likewise, the death instinct, in Freud's view, aims for "not just *any kind* of death, but a particular death" that will achieve this same return to a tensionless, inorganic state.[2] There is, then, a symmetry between the sex instinct and the death instinct.

The second reason it is important to understand Freud's point of view has to do with our intuitive response to his claims about the instincts. Thanks largely to Freud, we are now quite accustomed to the idea that sexuality is important psychologically for the tasks of living. But we might also find his apparent monomaniacal focus on sexuality both reductive and repellent. Similarly, the proposition of a primary drive toward death or dissolution strikes us, as it struck even Freud's closest followers, as weirdly counterintuitive. But an examination of how Freud developed these concepts and why he gave them such a central place in his theory provides, I believe, a window into some apparent existential truths about the human condition, even though Freud's approach was often unorthodox and beyond the canons of science even broadly defined. In any case, the depiction of that human condition in *Civilization* makes no sense without them.

SEX

can't get no . . . satisfaction

—Jagger and Richards

Sex, for Freud, is not about merely the biological mechanics of reproduction, nor is reproduction its sole aim. At bottom, sexual activity is directed toward *tension reduction,* the release of organic and psychic tension. Tension reduction, in turn, is related to the "principle of constancy," the tendency of an organism to maintain equilibrium or homeostasis. Finally, Freud's thinking about tension reduction and psychological homeostasis was firmly rooted in the reflex tradition, which goes back to Descartes and was a dominant heuristic in the physiology laboratory. In this view, the organism achieves tension reduction by making responses that rid it of irritation created by both external and internal stimuli. Descartes offered the classic example of a human reflexive response: the withdrawal of a hand from a flame.

This reflex tradition was central to Freud's thinking about how human organisms move through their worlds: "Reflex processes," he said, "remain the model of every psychical function" (*Interpretation*, 538). But this does not mean that Freud viewed human beings simply as reflex machines, nor does it follow that sex, for Freud, is simply a reflex response. Rather, Freud equated tension reduction with pleasure, and in his view it is the pleasure principle that "dominates the operation of the mental apparatus from the start." "[T]he purpose of life is simply the programme of the pleasure principle," he stated (25). Of course Freud understood that sexual activity could also be directed toward reproduction and argued that within advantageous developmental contexts, mature sexual behavior would (and should) culminate in genital intercourse.[3] He told his audiences time and again, however, that they were "committing the error of confusing sexuality and reproduction" if they believed that sex was restricted to heterosexual intercourse.[4]

If the idea of sex as tension reduction seems overly simple and reductive, we must understand what tension reduction means for human beings as they develop. Unlike the simple case of the child moving her hand away from the flame, the unpleasant situations that human beings encounter over the course of a life create much more complex problems and conflicts. It is the multiplicity of these problems and conflicts that Freud has in mind when, in *Civilization*, he argues that unhappiness is inevitable for human beings. Thus Freud's claims about the nature of the psychic apparatus and the world it encounters and grows into lead in two different directions. On the one hand, his conceptualization of sexuality links basic physiological processes to the simple idea of pleasure as tension reduction. But on the other hand, it also leads upward toward a much fuller conception of sexuality than our common one, incorporating even existential themes. To see how Freud achieves this, we must examine more closely the concept of instinct, or drive, for Freud used it in a distinctive and important way.

In German, there are two equivalents of the English word *instinct,* and Freud used each in specific ways. The first, *Instinkt,* refers to the kind of instincts found in both human beings and animals that are relatively fixed in nature, are entirely a function of heredity, and vary little from one member of a species to another.[5] The example of a child withdrawing her hand from a flame is an example of *Instinkt.* The various tropisms we see in the animal kingdom, such as insects moving toward a nutrient source, are other examples.

Freud was aware that a good deal of human behavior could be understood in the context of this first kind of instinct. A newborn suckling at the mother's breast might be considered an example of instinct in this sense, in the same way that we would classify as instinctive a robin regurgitating worms for its fledglings. But this is where the complexity begins, because the child suckling at the mother's breast is, in Freud's view, not only instinctual in this first sense but also "the prototype of every relation of love."[6] And love, or Eros, is, most importantly for Freud, a prime mover of civilization, which means that the sex instinct in this sense cannot be something fixed and unchanging. *Instinkt* alone is simply not sufficient to propel all the work that needs to be done in the Freudian world.

The second German word for instinct is *Trieb,* and Freud employed it to explore a much more flexible variety of instinct. *Trieb* comes closer to the idea of a drive—an energy pushing the organism in a particular direction—although even this equivalent is not sufficient. *Trieb* connotes a process that is both dynamic and malleable. Like *Instinkt,* its aim is tension reduction, but the aim is much more complex because it can be satisfied in a number of ways depending on the state of the organism, its developmental stage, its history, and the particular objects that are available to achieve or attempt that satisfaction (Laplanche and Pontalis). In a sense important to Freud, *Trieb* has a *fate* or an end that depends on the interaction of all these variables.

It is also important to keep in mind that for Freud, this much more nuanced and complex idea of instinct is not the bodily energy itself but rather its psychical representative. As he referred to it in the series of papers on metapsychology he wrote between 1914 and 1917, instinct—*Trieb*—is an entity that exists on the frontier between soma and psyche. While it is true that, like all of our relatives in the animal kingdom who use sex to reproduce, we have sexual *Instinkt,* what is crucial for understanding Freud is that we also possess sexual *Trieb* and that, in a real way, this dynamic instinct possesses us: "[W]e are 'lived' by unknown and uncontrollable forces."[7] It is in this sense that Freud's claim about our sexual nature takes on meaning.

Immediately after birth, the infant is a sexual creature because he is seeking to reestablish through an oral route the tensionless state that has been lost by being separated from the mother.[8] This aim of recovering something essential that has been lost is the most important element of the sex instinct (*Trieb*). If we were not faced with this loss by the very fact of our birth, the sex instinct in Freud's sense would not exist, and we would not have his account of the development of civilization.[9] For the infant, of course, suckling may reduce this hunger, but only temporarily. All of our sexual acts are motivated by this sense of incompleteness and loss that is part and parcel of the ephemeral satisfactions they may bring. The paradox is that if these acts did not have this incompleteness built in we would not engage in them in the first place, for it is the very tension of incompleteness that sets them in motion.

Freud was well aware that he might be labeled a pansexualist, as he was by both friend and foe. He rejected this label, and rightly so. In his first theory of the instincts, he distinguished between the sexual instincts and the self-preservative instincts. While self-preservation is obviously an important motivating force, it is only the sex instincts that aim for tension reduction, or pleasure. The self-preservative instincts, on the other hand, follow the reality principle and aim to carry the organism through the life cycle.[10] Notice that while these two aims might seem intertwined at the level of *Instinkt*—sexual activity is one of the many mechanisms that an organism uses in a reflexive way to ensure the survival both of itself and its species—they are clearly separable at the level of *Trieb*: at this level, sex is for pleasure, not survival. The later instinct theory that we see in *Civilization* brings both pleasure and self-preservation under the umbrella of Eros. In this final conception, all of our productive work, including that which helps increase our chances for survival, is, broadly speaking, sexual or erotic.

For Freud, the connection between the infant suckling at the breast and the many creative acts that together create and sustain civilization is clear and direct. Because the sex instinct is something more in the nature of a dynamic process than a simple reflex, though one intimately related to our biological being, this instinct manifests itself in very different ways depending on the individual's stage of development. Thus Freud called the first period of psychosexual development the oral stage, to indicate that the mouth is, at this period of life, the primary zone of organ pleasure—that is, it is an erotogenic zone. As development continues, other parts of the body are transformed into erotogenic zones, and so Freud spoke of the anal stage, the phallic stage, and the genital stage. These stages differ insofar as the primary erotogenic zone changes in each, but what they share is, once again, the goal of the pleasure principle: the mastery and control of stimuli.

But just as the aim of the sex instinct remains constant while the route of expression changes in an orderly, developmental fashion, the way in which the instinct is expressed changes over the course of a life. These changes are a response to the barriers, both within the psyche and outside it, that are constructed against the instinct. Freud referred to the multiple alterations that the instincts undergo as *Triebschicksale,* which literally means the fate or destiny of the drives. The translation that has been adopted, however, is "vicissitudes," a word that nicely captures what Freud intended: the sense in which the instincts, over the course of a life, undergo various changes or mutations, in part as a natural process but also as a way of responding to exigency (Ananke in *Civilization*) by making ad hoc substitutions.[11] Thus, in addition to the primary zone of pleasure shifting over the course of development, so does the instinct itself undergo such vicissitudes as "reversal into its opposite ... turning round upon the subject's own self ... repression [and] sublimation."[12]

It is through the process of instincts being transformed vicissitudinally, as it were, that all of the products of civilization come into being. A key element of Freud's theory is the transformation of the low into the high. The "much trampled soil from which our virtues proudly spring" is essentially the soil of the instincts and their vicissitudes (*Interpretation,* 621). In regard to the sex instincts, this helps us to understand why Freud could refer to children as "polymorphously perverse" (*Three Essays,* 191): during the course of psychosexual development, instincts will undergo vicissitudes in relation to any one of the erotogenic zones, which will alter the individual's propensity to seek organ pleasure through this end. This formulation also helps us understand Freud's claim that no single piece of sexual behavior, in isolation, can be considered either "perverse" or "normal." Although Freud had a very firm sense of what constitutes psychosexual health in the individual—namely, all of the component instincts that are associated with each erotogenic zone coming under the umbrella, in the adult, of heterosexual intercourse—he also argued that this is very difficult to achieve and that a good deal of our erotic life is improvisational. We are polymorphous, it seems, even when we are not perverse, and the variety of forms that the expressions of instincts take is also responsible for the products of civilization.[13]

So although as animals we are sexual creatures in the simple sense of using sex to reproduce, being a sexual creature in Freud's sense means something deeper and more complex. The pleasure principle that figures so prominently in *Civilization* is no frivolous thing. This deep sense of sexuality has more to do with the "Eros of the divine Plato" than with our animal natures (*Three Essays,* 134). In essence, it marks us as pilgrims, though Freud himself might not have tolerated such language.[14] We are in search of something we once had but, by virtue of being human, necessarily had to lose.

THE DEATH INSTINCT

... a consummation devoutly to be wished

—Shakespeare

Get back ... get back to where you once belonged
—Lennon and McCartney

That Freud would further emphasize the theme of loss, so central to understanding our sexual strivings, as his theory continued to grow and develop is hinted at in the last of the *Three Essays:* "There are good reasons why a child sucking at his mother's breast has become the prototype of every relation of love. The finding of an object is in fact a refinding of it" (88). Freud is suggesting that the shape relationships take later in our lives is constrained by the crucial early years of our development. Put another way, part of *every* relationship in life is an attempt to reestablish an earlier state of affairs. It is this notion of attempting to return to or reestablish something once enjoyed that lies at the core of the concept of the death instinct, just as it does for the sex instinct. In *Beyond the Pleasure Principle,* Freud revealed, by way of providing a working definition, that the idea of the death instinct had also led to a fundamental shift in the theory of instincts in general: "*It seems then, that an instinct is an urge inherent in organic life to restore an earlier state of things* which the living entity has been obliged to abandon under the pressure of external disturbing forces" (*Beyond,* 36; italics in original). At the center of things, then, lies the same aim that underlies the sex instinct, namely tension reduction. As we shall see, there are further parallels between the sex and death instincts. Before getting to these complexities, though, I must deal with two preliminaries.

First, although *Civilization* argues that aggression is the chief manifestation of the death instinct, it cannot be too strongly emphasized that this aggression, in Freud's view, is a derivative of the death instinct, not the reverse. Just as there are misconceptions about what Freud really meant by sex, we misread Freud when we take him to say that we desire death in the simple sense of demise. While one might be able to construct a theory of aggression on the premise of some kind of suicidal impulse, this is not what Freud had in mind.[15] When human aggression is viewed to be itself the outgrowth of something more basic to the human condition, we arrive at a very different sense of what this aggression is. The Freudian death instinct has more to do, at its core, with repetition and mastery than with aggression per se, although it remains true that aggression is a "vicissitude" of the death instinct. The main point, which bears repeating, is that the death instinct comes first.

Second, there is the question of why Freud put so much emphasis, in his later years of theory building, 1919 to 1926 and through the completion of *Civilization,* on the death instinct and its main derivative. Remembering Freud's personal tribulations during these years—notably, the death of his daughter Sophie and his own battles with cancer—as well as the carnage of the Great War and its sequelae, it is tempting to conclude that all of these events led him to develop the concept. But although we can allow that Freud's preoccupation with his own mortality and his temperament more generally might have predisposed him to the emphasis he gave to both the death instinct and its main derivative, there are significant vectors within the theory itself that make the concept of the death instinct, at least in retrospect, appear inevitable.[16] Let us turn to some of these vectors now.

As he tells us in *Beyond,* Freud had long been troubled by how to account for anxiety dreams within the boundaries of the pleasure principle: to put it simply, anxiety dreams just aren't pleasurable experiences. Of course one could, and Freud did—in *Interpretation* and in other writings—resort to the explanatory framework of the dynamic unconscious: anxiety dreams, while extremely unpleasant at the level of the manifest dream, might be disguising and defending against latent dream content that is pleasurable in the kind of primal and direct way that requires defense against it becoming conscious. In the "compromise formation" that grows out of this conflict, one sees a manifest content of anxiety.

But Freud found this kind of explanation inadequate in trying to make sense of the dreams and obsessional thoughts of soldiers returning from battle with traumatic neuroses. These dreams and thoughts "have the characteristic of repeatedly bringing the patient back into the situation of his accident" (*Beyond,* 13), and are difficult to reconcile along the lines of dreams as wish fulfillments and the "programme of the pleasure principle" (*Civilization,* 25). But if the foundation of such "return" is not pleasure, how does one make sense of it?

In attempting to answer this question, Freud turns to a discussion of children's play, using his observations of one of his grandson's games:

> The child had a wooden reel with a piece of string tied around
> it.... What he did was to hold the reel by the string and very skil-
> fully throw it over the edge of the curtained cot, so that it disap-
> peared into it, at the same time uttering his expressive "o-o-o-o."
> He then pulled the reel out of the cot again by the string and
> hailed its reappearance with a joyful "*da*" ["there"]. This, then,
> was the complete game—*disappearance and return.* (*Beyond,* 15;
> my emphasis)

The connection Freud makes between this game and the dreams of the
traumatic neuroses is that in both cases there is a return to an unpleasurable event. In the childhood game, Freud supposes, the child is
staging a reenactment of the disappearance and return of his mother.
Although this reenactment does have a pleasurable aspect alongside
the unpleasurable theme of disappearance, namely the return of the
mother, Freud wonders whether this feature of childhood games—the
repetition of events with the aim of mastering them—might help us
understand what is going on in the traumatic neuroses.

Freud then tells us that this "compulsion to repeat" is also a necessary component of successful therapy. In transference, the patient
begins to reenact with the analyst material from the past that is
repressed. It would be preferable, perhaps, and less emotionally draining if the patient could simply remember this repressed material and
learn from it. But this does not happen; an actual repetition seems
necessary:

> The patient cannot remember the whole of what is repressed in
> him, and what he cannot remember may be precisely the essential
> part of it.... He is obliged to *repeat* the repressed material as a
> contemporary experience instead of, as the physician would pre-
> fer to see, *remembering* it as something belonging to the past.
> (*Beyond,* 18, italics in original)

Finally, Freud observes that there are many instances, even in normal
life, when we seem plagued by the " 'perpetual recurrence of the same
thing' ":

> Thus we have come across people all of whose human relationships
> have the same outcome: such as the benefactor who is abandoned

in anger time after time by each of his *protégés* ... or the man whose friendships all end in betrayal by his friend. (*Beyond*, 22)

All these phenomena of "return" move Freud to conclude "that there really does exist in the mind a compulsion to repeat which overrides the pleasure principle"—the death instinct (*Beyond*, 22).

As Fancher has discussed, Freud's adoption of the concept of the death instinct allowed him to smooth out a big bump in the theory of the instincts as it had developed up to this point. At the time he formulated the libido theory, Freud felt comfortable making a distinction between sex instincts and ego instincts. The former followed the pleasure principle and were aimed at satisfaction through attachment to various sexual objects, as I described in the last section. The ego instincts, on the other hand, followed the reality principle and aimed not for satisfaction but for self-preservation. But this distinction between sex and self-preservative instincts was blurred by Freud's observations of narcissism, or self-love, since it involves one's self, or ego, as a love object.

The concept of narcissism is crucial to understanding the view presented in *Civilization*. By introducing this concept, Freud was able to make the important connection between love of self and love of others. It is through the concept of narcissism that Freud was able to explore how these concentrically arranged spheres of libidinal attachment—self, love object, then outward beyond the bonds of the family—form the base of the social cohesion that is at once a building block of civilization and a source of unhappiness, since the construction of social cohesion demands renunciation of the libidinal ties at the center of the circle.

The concept of narcissism, however, also destroys the distinction between sex and self-preservative instincts, because with it comes the claim that ego drives are sexual, too. By introducing the concept of the death instinct, Freud achieved two goals. First, he was able to say that the concept of libido was not so general as to be useless—a kind of pansexualism, as Carl Jung had charged. Even though both the sex instinct and the death instinct have the aim of tension reduction, only the sex instinct takes the route of the pleasure principle. Second, the introduction of the death instinct gave Freud's theory the simplicity he always sought. Now both classes of instincts could be seen as regressive, or aimed at tension reduction, while at the same time restoring a polarity or duality—formerly between the sex instincts and the self-preservative or ego instincts, now between the life instincts and the death instincts—that had been blurred by the concept of narcissism. In *Civilization,* Freud admits to his attachment to this new formulation on purely aesthetic lines: "To my mind, [these views] are far more serviceable from a theoretical standpoint than any other possible ones; they provide the simplification, without either ignoring or doing violence to the facts, for which we strive in scientific work" (79).

In Freud's view, the death instinct is also essential for the development of civilization because it is the source of our attempts at mastery, the inclination to which is also seen through the repetition compulsion. For example,

> Order is a kind of compulsion to repeat which, when a regulation has been laid down once and for all, decides when, where and how a thing shall be done, so that in every similar circumstance one is spared hesitation and indecision. The benefits of order are incontestable. (46)

I have already emphasized the point that this Freudian death is characterized not chiefly by demise but rather by a return to an inorganic state of nirvana. But along the way, the death instinct undergoes various vicissitudes and transformations, just like the sex instinct. Human beings achieve the flowering of civilization while at the instinctual level simply trying to master and take control of troubling events in a way that parallels what Freud saw in the traumatic neuroses and the play of his grandson.

Once the death instinct is clarified in this way, we see its complete functional equivalence to Eros. For both Eros and death, the aim is to reestablish a lost satisfaction. Via the route of sexuality, this tensionless state is achieved in sexual union, but this sexual union is, in Freud's view, nothing but a kind of paradise regained. Via the route of death, the tensionless state is achieved through dissolution, not paradise, but nevertheless just as much as sexual union, a "consummation devoutly to be wished."

The most important derivatives of Eros have to do with con-structive tasks at levels ranging from artistic creativity to the structures and processes that make an orderly civilization possible, from the libidinal ties of a loving couple to the social cohesion that undergirds those structures and processes. The most important derivative of the death instinct, by contrast, is aggression, which also operates at more than one level: directed outward, it creates the kind of violence that is one reason civilization is necessary; directed inward, it gives impetus to the force of the super-ego, itself one of the products as well as one of the instigators of civilization.

The death instinct retains its status as especially bizarre, even compared to other Freudian concepts. However, it must be asked: despite the fact that Freud's argument for the death instinct is often contradicted by visible evidence, and despite the fact that it strains credulity, might it nevertheless hold some value in thinking about the dilemmas of the human condition?

In posing this question, I have in mind other frameworks for understanding human aggression. For more than 50 years, the explo-ration of human aggression from a psychological point of view has been dominated by two contrasting approaches, which Erich Fromm labeled the environmentalist and the instinctivist approaches.[17]

Simply put, the environmentalist approach, associated with the behaviorism of B. F. Skinner, seeks to understand aggression by look-ing at factors in the outside world, external to the person, that shape and reinforce aggressive behavior. In the environmentalist model, there is little need to take into account what the person is like on the inside in terms of drives, instincts, and the like. The behaviorist argues that we can account for and understand, at least in principle, enough about human aggression by focusing on these external factors without worrying about biological ones. Although the heyday of such a simple and monolithic behavioral approach is past, having been superseded in psychology by the revolutions in cognitive science and neuroscience, the behavioral point of view remains influential. For example, in our attempt to understand violent behavior in children, we often call upon the concepts of modeling and vicarious learning, which make these behavioralist assumptions.

The instinctivist approach, on the other hand, holds that human aggression can be understood only by employing the very concept of instinct that the behaviorist believes can be overlooked. In the 1950s and 1960s, the instinctivist approach was most clearly associated with the work of Konrad Lorenz and other ethologists. In general terms, the instinctivist works within the framework of Darwinian theory and makes the assumption that any persistent behavioral trait must have survival value for the organism or it would not have been carried down through the generations. The movement called sociobiology, associated with the writings of E. O. Wilson and Richard Dawkins, operates within this framework and claims that human aggression can be understood only by taking into account its similarity to aggression in other animals.[18]

To a considerable extent, such a biological view makes sense, and it is one to which Freud adhered in his own work. As we have seen, in his early theory of the instincts Freud conceptualized the ego instincts as self-preservative and included aggression among them. Essentially all of the aggression that we observe outside of the human domain can be understood in terms of survival mechanisms—such as territoriality and protection of offspring—which make sense in Darwinian terms. Even the killing of offspring, outside of the human realm, has survival value for the organisms that exhibit it.

Clearly, though, human aggression is more complex, and it is here that Freud's concept of the death instinct may be of service. Ironically, one of the arguments that Freud used to defend his concept was that the death instincts exist in other animals, too: for example, salmon return to the site of their birth and then die. Remember, his claim was that *all* organic life exhibits such an instinct, and this claim is surely wrong. But what about human beings?

To be sure, some of the aggressive behavior that we see in human beings can be understood in terms of Darwinian principles. I would fight—and kill, I hope—to defend the lives of my children. And on a political level, an aspect of war is territoriality, the motivation to protect self-interest. But having said this, the issue becomes more complicated, and we move into a domain in which the Freudian view becomes more useful than the Darwinian one.

The problem is that much of human aggression is not what Fromm calls "benign aggression," directed toward self-preservation, but instead qualifies as "malignant aggression." As Fromm puts it, "[T]here is hardly a destructive act human imagination could think of that has not been acted out again and again" (271). In addition to protecting ourselves against foes, we also torture one another, exhibit cruelty toward members of both our own and other species, and kill when doing so is clearly not sensible from a Darwinian standpoint. As Fromm implies, a list of such malignantly aggressive acts would be infinitely long, so long that we begin to wonder whether, in the human realm, malignant aggression isn't far more common than benign aggression.

Moving from aggression between individuals to examples in the world of geopolitics, a similar picture emerges. As I write this chapter in the winter of 1996, the world watches as the Irish Republican Army ends its 17-month cease-fire by detonating a powerful bomb in the Docklands section of London. The British government has so far responded by insisting that the IRA lay down its arms before peace negotiations can begin, in effect demanding surrender. And in Bosnia, we see the very kind of civil war that is, sadly, not new to this globe inhabited by human beings, the kind of strife that led Freud pessimistically to talk about the "narcissism of minor differences" and its consequences (*Civilization*, 72).

While all such political confrontations may in part reflect straightforward issues having to do with self-interest, what they share is that they cannot be very well understood by resorting primarily, or much at all, to simple notions of self-preservation. Scanning the historical record, one is impressed by how this malignant aggression seems to have much more to do with a desire to restore a state of affairs that once existed, whether in reality or in the imagination, an imagination itself either benign or malignant. Hitler's program to restore an Aryan race; the desire of the South, in America's Civil War, to maintain an agrarian way of life: these are, to be sure, very different examples, and only two, but what they show, like any number of other examples could, is that human aggression cannot be at all well understood in a simple instinctivist framework. Something more convoluted is called for, an idea that encompasses not only humankind's propensity toward polymorphous perversity but also polymorphous aggression and cruelty, not only to others but to ourselves.

At several points in his writings, Freud called attention to the idea that the sex and death instincts are alloyed, that in some sense their fates are bound together. Having now surveyed the territory, it is interesting to look back and see how very much they indeed have in common.

First, it is clear that both instincts have aims. Further, although only the sex instinct follows the route of the pleasure principle, the aim for both is tension reduction, the mastery and control of unsettling, nirvana-destroying stimulation. In more existential terms, they both aim for that ever-elusive recapture or return to an Edenic state that is lost by virtue of being made human.

Second, although Freud said that he could speak specifically only of the vicissitudes the sexual instincts undergo, the death instinct also has this transformational nature. Of course, with the vicissitudinal nature of these instincts of life and death come all sorts of problems, but they are parallel in an intriguing way. Just as only human beings are polymorphously perverse, only human beings are polymorphously cruel. Cruelty is to the death instinct as perversion is to the sex instinct.

If there would be no civilization without sexuality, neither would there be civilization without the death instinct. Norman O. Brown captured this Freudian fact of life in the most poetic way that I have encountered. "History," he said, "is a forward-moving *recherche du temps perdu,* with the repetition-compulsion guaranteeing the historical law of the slow return of the repressed."[19] Without a transformed sex instinct, we would be locked in some autoerotic or boundariless condition, which may sound like fun until we realize that we would not be conscious of it in any sense: Eros really is a motor of psychic life. But without a transformed death instinct, we would, in an existential sense, never emerge from the slime from which we came. This, too, would solve the problem of tension reduction, but once again, it wouldn't be much fun. So to paraphrase Mick Jagger and Keith Richards, not only can we never get what we really want, it is only because we can't ever get it that we have anything at all: perversion and cruelty, yes, but also love, the internal compulsion of ethics, and more.

5

The Unconscious:
Dynamic, Conflictual, Transformative

The unconscious is the true psychical reality; *in its innermost nature it is as much unknown to us as the reality of the external world, and it is as incompletely presented by the data of consciousness as is the external world by the communications of our sense organs.*
—Freud, *The Interpretation of Dreams;* italics in original

How can there be an animal which represses itself?
—Norman O. Brown, Life against Death

In the Freudian view, there would be nothing without the instincts—no conscious experience, no civilization. But the instincts by themselves are insufficient for the development of psychological life and culture. This is the paradox that Freud puts at the center of *Civilization:* while we can never be fully at home in civilization because of the instinctual renunciation it demands, it is this very renunciation that makes civilization, as well as all the other products of our psychological lives, possible. At one and the same time, we can admit that "it is impossible to overlook the extent to which civilization is built upon a renunciation of instinct, how much it presupposes precisely the non-satisfaction (by suppression, repression, or some other means?) of powerful instincts" but also that this work of building culture is one that binds all psychological energies together in the best available way (51–52). The work of culture demands renunciation, but out of this renunciation comes a transformation of the raw energy of the instincts into products of utility and beauty: "Where id was, there ego shall be. It is a work of culture—not unlike the draining of the Zuider Zee" (*NIL*, 80).

Renunciation. Suppression. Repression. Transformation. All of these processes, in Freud's view, are carried out by a dynamic unconscious whose modus operandi is conflict. Just as we cannot appreciate Freud's ideas about humankind's predicament in culture without understanding the nature of the instincts that propel us forward (and backward), we cannot appreciate his claims about the instincts without understanding the unconscious processes through which they are transformed into things known. Without such an unconscious, instincts would not undergo their many vicissitudes, and without such processes, we would not be human, for what makes us human in his view is not instinct itself—all animals are instinctual—but its transformation.

At one level, the idea of a dynamic unconscious does not strike us as nearly as counterintuitive or repellent as Freud's claims about the nature of instinctual life. The metaphor of the mind as an iceberg, with the interesting part submerged below the waterline, is one that many of us have encountered, and we take for granted that part of human motivation operates outside of conscious awareness.

At another level, however, Freud's claims for the primacy of unconscious psychological life are every bit as revolutionary as his claims for the instincts. For in his view, nothing above the waterline contributes significantly to either our motivations or our understanding of them. As Freud's views on the nature of the unconscious evolved, from his first conceptualization of two conflictual mental agencies to the model that is most familiar to us, the tripartite scheme of id, ego, and super-ego, the claim that the unconscious is the true psychical reality only became stronger and more compelling.

Freud's path toward the idea of a dynamic and conflictual unconscious that creates conscious entities began in his work with patients suffering from hysteria. Hysteria has a long and controversial history. Literally, it means "from the uterus," and although physicians in the late nineteenth century no longer believed that its symptoms were caused by a wandering womb, it was still "considered a strange disease with incoherent and incomprehensible symptoms" and associated far more often with women than with men.[1] At the core of hysteria is a symptom for which there is no discernible organic cause. Even today, when a patient comes to a physician with vague complaints that do not point to a clear organic base, there is some tendency, though certainly less than a century ago, to believe that the patient is malingering or simply making it up. And while it is important to stress that Freud did not simply invent the concept of a dynamic unconscious—it has a long and complex history—that we are much more disposed to treat psychological distress as real than we were a century ago is certainly part of his legacy.

Freud's work with Charcot in Paris and later with Breuer in Vienna convinced him that while hysterical symptoms by definition are not accompanied by an underlying organic problem, they are nevertheless caused by entities that have structure, logic, and meaning; they are caused by ideas. This recognition is a cornerstone of the Freudian revolution. In a scientific paper based on his work in Paris, Freud makes a compelling case for taking seriously the causal role of ideas—their ability to cause both behavioral and organic symptoms, certainly a reversal of the normally conceived casual stream.[2]

In this paper, Freud compares the symptoms observed in organic paralysis with those observed in hysterical paralysis. The former point to clear evidence of organic damage; the latter indicate no such evidence. The symptoms differ in other ways as well. In organic paralysis, Freud says, "there is not the slightest doubt as to the conditions which dominate the symptomatology.... They are the facts of anatomy—the construction of the nervous system and the distribution of its vessels."[3] Because the symptoms are dominated by these "facts of anatomy," they are incomplete and messy. For example, the loss of feeling (anesthesia) that often accompanies organic paralysis is incomplete relative to our idea of, say, an arm or a limb; the loss of feeling is spotty, confined to a portion of the limb and spreading to adjacent areas of the body. This is so because the symptoms are entirely correlated with the distribution of nerves, which supply not just an entire arm or a region of the arm but an area of the body. So in an organic paralysis, the affected portions of the body never correspond very well to the idea or concept of an arm, a leg, or the like.

In hysterical paralysis, however, the situation is quite different. For example, in "glove anaesthesia" we find that the entire hand and wrist, and only these areas, are afflicted. In short, the symptoms in this case correspond to the idea of a body part rather than to a pattern of nerve distribution. For this reason, Freud was able to assert that the damage in "hysterical paralyses must be completely independent of the nervous system, since *in its paralyses and other manifestations hysteria behaves as though anatomy did not exist or as though it had no knowledge of it*" ("Comparative Study," 169; italics in original).

Although the symptoms are ignorant, as it were, of the facts of anatomy, they are nevertheless imbued with meaning on a psychological level. Nowhere was this more compellingly shown than in the case of "Anna O."[4] The case study was written by Breuer, who had treated Anna in the 1880s. In Breuer's words, the case contains "the germ of the whole of psychoanalysis" (quoted in Gay 1988, 64). Anna was a young woman suffering from a variety of symptoms, including a severe cough, a squint that impaired her vision, and paralysis and anesthesia. While she was always able to understand her native German, she experienced episodes in which she could speak only in English. As her treatment with Breuer progressed, she also developed hydrophobia, an inability to drink water, and "a feeling of revulsion ... whenever she brought a glass near her lips" (Fancher, 49).

The case of Anna O. was an "epoch-making collaboration between a gifted patient and her attentive physician" (Gay 1988, 65), both because of what they learned and how they learned it. Over the course of Breuer and Anna's relationship, it became clear that all of Anna's symptoms revolved around traumatic memories of caring for her dying father. For example, her squint and visual impairment were connected to a memory of sitting by her father's bedside, trying to hold back tears at the realization of his deteriorating condition. Similarly, the episodes in which her speaking was restricted to English were traced back to a panic-stricken state in which she repeated over and over the words of an English prayer.

All of these connections were discovered through the simple process of Anna talking out loud during hypnotic states that were for the most part self-induced in Breuer's presence. What was important was that the original traumatic scene be reexperienced with a good measure of its original emotional intensity. Breuer and Freud called this process *abreaction,* and it now holds an essential place in psycho-analytic therapy. During abreaction, the memory is brought to con-sciousness and the symptom disappears. Anna herself described this process as "chimney sweeping" and the therapy as "the talking cure." Later, Freud would abandon hypnosis for the process of free associa-tion, leaving behind the many complications of an induced hypnotic state but keeping the central part of this talking cure, namely the "adoption of an attitude of uncritical self-observation" that allows these unconscious ideas to emerge (*Interpretation,* 103).

Freud's exploration of hysterical paralyses convinced him that symptoms that have no organic base are nevertheless real and mean-ingful; they are caused by ideas. The case of Anna O. showed him that these symptoms emerge out of the struggle between unconscious ideas and a censoring agency that tries to deny them access to conscious-ness. In Freud's scheme, these unconscious ideas, in their undisguised form, created unpleasure; the censorship was an attempt to transform those unconscious ideas into something merely more palatable or less painful (in the case of a symptom, which is created by the process of repression) and perhaps even useful (in the case of the work of civi-lization, which is largely the work of sublimation). For example, in the case of Anna O., the symptom of distorted vision, while surely unpleasant, was much less so than the idea of her father's death. Thus Anna's tears in the original situation become symbolically linked to the symptom of blurred vision.

"If Freud's discovery had to be summed up in a single word, that word would without doubt have to be 'unconscious' " (Laplanche and Pon-talis, 474). So far in this chapter, I have been discussing Freud's con-cept of a dynamic and conflictual unconscious as if it were a unitary concept. But just like his thinking about the instincts, Freud's under-standing of the unconscious evolved over the course of his life. In this section, I follow Laplanche and Pontalis in talking about the first and second "topographies." The first topography, which developed out of Freud's early collaboration with Charcot, Fliess, and Breuer, empha-sized the conflictual relationship between a wishful, sexual, infantile unconscious and a defensive agency. The second topography refers to the well-known tripartite scheme of id, ego, and super-ego. We shall see that these two topographies are interrelated in important ways.[5]

It is more than pedantic to recall that Freud used the word *unconscious* as both an adjective and a noun. As a noun, it refers to a system and, in the first topography, metaphorically to a region of the mind. As an adjective, Freud used it primarily to describe all of the processes, generally defensive in nature, that characterize so much of

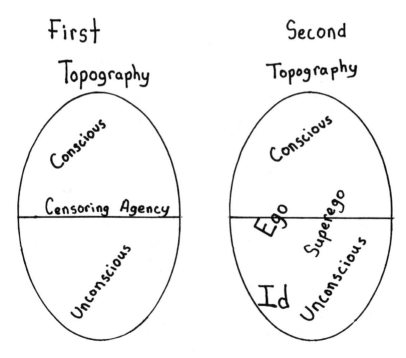

Ben Parisi

mental work. But even in its adjectival sense, *unconscious* is less a descriptor of the psychological work itself than of "where" in the psychic apparatus it takes place. The essence of the work itself is its conflictual dynamism: for all of its importance,

> the characteristic of being unconscious begins to lose significance for us. It becomes a quality which can have many meanings, a quality which we are unable to make, as we should have hoped to do, the basis of far-reaching and inevitable conclusions.

Still, the concept's central importance, in both its grammatical forms, remains: "[W]e must beware of ignoring this characteristic, for the property of being conscious or not is in the last resort our one beacon-light in the darkness of depth-psychology" (*EI,* 18).

Even while generating these topographies, or structures, of the mind, Freud was keenly aware of the problems inherent in attributing function to material "places" within the mind or brain. In *Interpretation,* for example, where Freud was most specifically interested in describing the psychic apparatus, he is careful to emphasize the dangers of trying to "determine psychical locality in any anatomical fashion" (536). And in *Civilization,* after developing the metaphor of the archaeology of Rome in some detail, he concludes by noting "how far we are from mastering the characteristics of mental life by representing them in pictorial terms" (19).

These distinctions between function and structure are further complicated by the fact that *unconscious* is also used to describe content. In Freud's first topography, the general process of repression or defense is brought to bear against the contents of the unconscious. But in this topography the way most of these unconscious contents become unconscious in the first place is through repression, which has the dual role of putting unconscious contents in place as well as keeping them there. Most of these contents, I emphasize, but not all. For Freud was careful to point out that there is more to the unconscious than what is put there by repression: "[T]he repressed does not cover everything in the unconscious. The unconscious has the wider compass: the repressed is *a part* of the unconscious."[6]

Some of these complications may be clarified by a description of the first and second topographies, their similarities, their differences, and their interrelationships.

The most important similarity is that in both systems, unconscious contents are transformed into conscious products by the various defense mechanisms. The functional essence of the psychic apparatus in both topographies is this dynamic conflict, the products of which are "compromise formations." All of the "deflections" and "substitutive satisfactions" that Freud lists in *Civilization* are such compromises (23–24). Work, love, intoxication, isolation, science, art: these are to varying degrees useful and satisfying, but even the best of them (work and love) fall short of the primal wishes from which they arise.

We can point as well to the most visible difference between the two topographies: the well-known entities of the id, ego, and super-ego are absent from the first topography but dominate the second. However, these two topographies coexist in Freud's theory. We can understand this apparent paradox by invoking Freud's idea of "preservation in the sphere of the mind" (16), which he communicated with the metaphor of Rome as archaeological site. The tripartite structural scheme in the second topography does not replace the functional dynamics of the first. Rather, the two topographies are superimposed on each other, but neither claims developmental priority. The person reflecting on Freud's two topographies has "only to change the direction of his glance or his position in order to call up the one view or the other" (18).

The most common mistake in trying to reconcile the two topographies is to equate the unconscious with the id and then to assume that the ego and super-ego are conscious. Freud is himself partly responsible for this blurring, since the first topography portrays an instinctual unconscious held in check by an oppositional, repressive agency. That the functional pivot point of the tripartite model is unconscious, however, becomes clear as soon as one realizes that the defense against unconscious urges must itself be unconscious, since we know only its effects. In the second topography, then, the id is entirely unconscious, but the ego and super-ego also have unconscious regions, and it is in this nether nexus that psychological life is worked out.

Thus the mind of the second topography is more richly dynamic than the mind of the first topography. While the essential tension between the unconscious and a censoring agency remains, complications arise because the ego must now serve "three tyrannical masters" (NIL, 77): while trying to meet the demands of the id according to its own rules (the reality principle), it must negotiate not only the outside world but also the harsh requirements of the super-ego.

With the articulation of the second topography, Freud was also able to clarify what unconscious material consists of. First there is the id, a "chaos, a cauldron full of seething excitations" (NIL, 73). The id consists both of the instincts, which Freud emphasized are not the somatic impulses themselves but their ideational representatives, and of phylogenetic memory traces that have never been part of individual conscious experience but that nevertheless constrain that experience. In addition to the id, there are the elements of personal experience that have been placed in the unconscious through the process of repression.

As Laplanche and Pontalis have noted, although the mind of the second topography, like that of the first, is dynamic and conflictual, there is also a discernible shift from mere conflict to a broad biological theme of differentiation and transformation. In this metaphorical picture, the ego and the super-ego owe their existence to the id, and all of their energy is appropriated from it. Indeed, the growth and differentiation of the mind in the second topography parallels Freud's depiction of the emergence and course of civilization. Like the mind, civilization too has its beginnings in instinctual life: "Where id was, there ego shall be" (NIL, 80).

It is clear, then, that there is an animal which represses itself; we are it.[7] But how can there be such an animal? In the world as depicted in *Civilization,* it seems clear why such repression is a given feature of human life: we possess impulses against which defense is necessary. And it is out of the conflict between the expression of these impulses and the defense against them that culture emerges. This is one sense in which necessity (Ananke) is a parent of civilization: such necessity is a response to a condition that already exists.

So to be human is to be continuously engaged in psychic conflict, a conflict that manifests itself not only at the individual level—in dreams, ambivalence, parapraxes, neurotic symptoms—but also at the communal level, in our attempts to "adjust the mutual relationships of human beings in the family, the state and society" (37). There is, however, another sense in which necessity is a parent of civilization beyond being brought into conflict with our instinctual passions in a merely reactive way. This brings us to the question raised by Norman Brown that serves as an epigraph to this chapter.

Sulloway makes the point that Freud was interested simultaneously in two different levels of explanation.[8] A proximate explanation is one given in terms of mere mechanism. At one level, Freud's explanation of civilization is simply a proximate one: civilization is created by the conflict between both internal and external demands and desire; it is made possible by the renunciation of instinct. An ultimate explanation, on the other hand, attempts to make sense of a phenomenon in terms of purpose; it goes beyond mere mechanism. Brown's question, though it begins with "how" rather than "why," is really asking for an ultimate explanation. Its meaning is not "How does the human animal repress itself?" but "Why is it that there is such an animal?"

From a Freudian perspective, a conflict model seems to be the only one that allows us to understand the human dilemma once it has reached a certain level of development. Once human beings are in a situation in which instinctual passions are struggling against the internal demands of the ego and super-ego and the external demands of nature and society, the kinds of mechanisms that keep this activity going seem self-evident. But how did we come to be in this situation in the first place? How can there be an animal which represses itself?

This question becomes important as soon as one recalls the nature of the instincts themselves. They are directed toward the discharge of tension, toward pleasure, toward nirvana. Why do any of these need to be defended against? Because conflict and renunciation are not simply responses to the instincts, which exist in some sort of ontologically prior state. Rather, conflict and renunciation are every bit as intrinsic to the human condition as the passions themselves; they have essentially the same ontological status as the instincts. From a developmental standpoint, we have something like an Aristotelian acorn. Necessity is a parent of civilization not only in the sense that the structures of civilization are necessary responses or reactions to the passions. Necessity is a parent also in the sense that civilization—or at least some kind of restrictive system that will demand renunciation—is inevitable by virtue of being human.

Implicit in the ultimate question is another: Could it have been different? Freud's answer is no: once we have a being that is human, the dynamic conflictual scheme of development is inevitable. Indeed, for Freud this is what it means to be human.

So how, in the Freudian world, does a human being become?[9] What makes us different from other animals? To be sure, we are truly and simply animals in one important respect—we possess instincts; as we have seen, Freud believed that all animals possessed a death instinct as well as sex instincts. In addition, Freud believed that other animals possessed something like an ego, although not in the dynamic sense in which it operates in human beings: "[N]o external vicissitudes can be experienced or undergone by the id, except by way of the ego, which is the representative of the external world to the id" (*EI*, 38). That is, the ego, in addition to its psychodynamic properties, is the portal through which any organism experiences the world.

But human beings are alone in the animal kingdom in being subject to the "cultural struggle" assayed in *Civilization* (83). Freud claims that "we do not know" why we are alone in this regard, but he is being forgetful here. There is, for Freud, a very specific ultimate reason, namely our evolutionary history. In his view, this history includes a particular event that set human beings on their course: the original Oedipal crime, the killing of the father. This primal act was followed by remorse, guilt, and totemic identification, and it was at this "moment when the human animal took the leap into civilization by prescribing to itself the taboos indispensable to all ordered societies" (Gay 1988, 324).

Freud's attachment to this idea of a specific historical event that marks the beginning of the history of civilization is problematic on two levels. First, the anthropological writings he relied on, including

Darwin's speculations about a primal horde, were both conjectural and unreliable. There is no evidence—none—for Freud's Oedipal scenario at the beginnings of human history. Second, Freud believed that the trace of this Oedipal event becomes part of the unconscious memory store of every individual, indeed the core of our "archaic remnant," through a process of biological inheritance. But this belief depends on the "inheritance of acquired characteristics," a view of evolution associated with Lamarck and now discredited. Indeed, the idea was discredited in Freud's own day, but like his stubborn embrace of a biological death instinct, he could not let it go:

> When I spoke of the survival of a tradition among a people or of the formation of a people's character, I had mostly in mind an inherited tradition of this kind and not one transmitted by communication. Or at least I made no distinction between the two and was not clearly aware of my audacity in neglecting to do so. My position, no doubt, is made more difficult by the present attitude of biological science, which refuses to hear of the inheritance of acquired characteristics by succeeding generations. I must, however, in all modesty confess that nevertheless I cannot do without this factor in biological evolution.[10]

Central to Freud's attachment to the idea of phylogenetic inheritance is the doctrine that "ontogeny recapitulates phylogeny," the claim that the development of the individual parallels the history of the entire species.[11] This is the claim that in the course of development, the individual repeats (i.e., recapitulates) the history of its adult ancestors. Like the inheritance of acquired characteristics, this "biogenetic law" has also been discredited, and we now understand that the resemblances we see among biological relatives—all vertebrates, for example—have more to do with shared ontogenies than with recapitulation.

Freud, then, was mistaken on two important counts. Today we do not accept the claim that characteristics that individuals acquire in their own lifetimes can be biologically transmitted to their offspring. Nor do we accept the claim that ontogeny recapitulates phylogeny. However, just as biologists remain interested "in the mechanisms by which phyletic information appears in ontogeny" despite the rejection of recapitulationist ideas (Gould, 3), Freud was interested in how the experience of past generations figures in the psychological development of the individual. And we can also note that, unlike the skepticism surrounding the inheritance of acquired characteristics, of which Freud was well aware, the inaccuracy of the claim that "ontogeny recapitulates phylogeny" was not nearly as appreciated in Freud's day and is still misunderstood in ours.

Furthermore, the linking of the idea of an ancestral primal scene with conjectures about its inheritance and persistence in memory grew seamlessly out of two currents. The "biogenetic law" was a very popular idea in Freud's day, and its main proponent, Haeckel, was the most influential purveyor of evolutionary ideas in Germany. So it is reasonable to expect that anyone who made an effort to keep up with developments in evolutionary biology, as Freud did, would imbibe recapitulation along with less problematic Darwinian ideas. But in addition to this current of biological thought, there was also the stream of Freud's clinical observations about the conservative nature of the instincts. In his clinical work, he saw, in broad strokes, the same general patterns of psychic conflict again and again.

And so when trying to devise not only a proximate explanation for what he observed in the human psyche but also an ultimate causal framework, Freud moved inexorably to the conclusion that "what is at bottom inherited is nevertheless *freshly acquired* in the development of the individual" (*Introductory Lectures,* 354–55; my italics). In each of our lives, we must fall victim to repression because of the constraint of the past, which is still powerfully operative in the present. We will, in each of our lives, find ourselves in situations of our own making. But this "own making" includes the active participation of both our ancestral and personal pasts.[12]

Thus Freud's answer to both questions—How can there be an animal which represses itself? and How does a human being become?—would have been, perhaps, simply "history." Trying to stay within the framework of his beloved scientific Weltanschauung, he tries to convince us that we can see human beings becoming by looking at the process of biological evolution through the lens of Haeckel's biogenetic law and of a Lamarckian idea of inheritance. While from our vantage point we can see that this framework by itself cannot sustain his claims about the nature of our humanity, of our persistent idiosyncrasies, or about civilization and our unease in it, we must also remember that Freud did not have access to the same intellectual equipment that is part of the late-twentieth-century Darwinian view of life. For Freud to be able to reject the notion that experiences of past generations can be inherited as unconscious memories, he would have had to accept the notion that the experiences of ancestors have nothing to do with behavior in the current generation. This he could not do—because of his personal inclinations but also because of what his clinical experience was telling him about the persistence of human foibles both within and across generations.

Much in the same way that the idea of a death instinct seems to make contact with a significant truth about human nature even as the concept defies satisfactory explanation within an empirical framework, Freud's claim that we are conflicted and self-repressive creatures—fractured, unwhole, unconsolable, a depiction in the final analysis not very different from those arising from Western religious and philosophical traditions—appears at least as compelling even as it, too, may finally elude scientific verification.

6

Ethics and the Place of Reason

The stars are indeed magnificent, but as regards conscience God has done an uneven and careless piece of work.

—Freud, *New Introductory Lectures on Psychoanalysis*

Self-love, the spring of motion, acts the soul;
Reason's comparing balance rules the whole.
Man, but for that, no action could attend,
And, but for this, were active to no end.

—Pope, "An Essay on Man"

It is sometimes argued that to try to draw moral lessons from nature is a mistake, and *Civilization* certainly provides food for thought when read simply as a natural history of humankind, as a description of our predicament rather than an evaluative or normative statement. The essay describes the Freudian organism in its milieu: fundamentally unconscious, moved simultaneously by erotic and morbid instincts, this is the tripartite organism of id, ego, and super-ego making its way in a world that is hostile in both natural and social terms.

In a letter to his friend Lou Andreas-Salomé, written on the day that he finished drafting *Civilization* at his summer retreat, Freud

58

seems to have confirmed the view that this text is merely an expository essay and further, that he penned it rapidly and without much of an agenda:

> It deals with civilization, sense of guilt, happiness, and similar exalted subjects, and strikes me, no doubt rightly, as quite superfluous in contrast to earlier works, which always sprang from some inner necessity. But what else can I do? One cannot smoke and play cards all day; I am no longer much good at walking, and most of what I read doesn't interest me anymore. I wrote, and in doing so the time passed quite pleasantly. While engaged in this work I have discovered the most banal truths.[1]

But Freud's attempt to minimize his own program is betrayed by the very first sentence of the essay itself: "It is impossible to escape the impression that people commonly use false standards of measurement ... and that they underestimate what is of true value in life" (10). While *Civilization* at one level describes the complications and contradictions of carrying out the functions of life in a Freudian world, at another level it gives us Freud's ideas about how we ought to live given the constraints of that world.

Freud achieved this ethical dimension by scrutinizing without sentimentality the world and human nature as he understood it. That is, he attempted to derive an ethical code by exploring the state of things. Freud wants to take seriously the idea that if we are to be about the business of building ethical systems, these systems must take into account what we know to be true about human nature. Otherwise they are doomed to worse than failure. And because Freud was confident in his views about the essence of human nature, he was also confident about the ethical prescriptions that he exhorted us to follow.

We shall see that Freud was not very far from the Aristotelian idea that a conclusion about the right way to live must derive from an understanding of the organism's proper function. But because the Freudian view of proper function has conflict—granted, transformative conflict—at its base, the Freudian ethic can seem correspondingly convoluted.

ETHICS AND SEXUALITY

I begin with Freud's ethical stance on sexuality because it can exemplify his point of view more generally. In *Three Essays,* Freud argued for two seemingly contradictory positions. He stated, on the one hand, that there is a particular way in which sexual development *should* proceed. Although the sex instinct is attached to different erotogenic zones, each of which exhibits primacy during different stages of psychosexual development, in the adult all components of the sexual instinct should come together under the umbrella of reproduction: "The final outcome of sexual development lies in what is known as the normal sexual life of the adult, in which the pursuit of pleasure comes under the sway of the reproductive function" (197). Simply put, "healthy" or "normal" development should lead to a particular outcome—heterosexuality directed toward reproduction.

At the same time, however, Freud argued that there is no one pattern of behavior that, in isolation, can be considered either normal or perverse. Because of the all-encompassing sense in which we are sexual creatures, our strivings toward satisfaction will manifest themselves in a great variety of ways. At the same time that Freud propounded a very conventional moral view about what should be the outcome of sexual development, he was also very clear that a great variety of sexual patterns and behaviors not only must be tolerated but are in fact necessary stopping points along the road to a fully mature sexuality:

> Everyday experience has shown that most of these extensions [of "normal" sexuality], or at any rate the less severe of them, are constituents which are rarely absent from the sexual life of healthy people.... No healthy person, it appears, can fail to make some addition that might be called perverse to the normal sexual aim; and the universality of this finding is in itself enough to show how inappropriate it is to use the word perversion as a term of reproach. In the sphere of sexual life we are brought up against peculiar and, indeed, insoluble difficulties as soon as we try to draw a sharp line to distinguish mere variations within the range

of what is physiological from pathological symptoms. (*Three Essays*, 160–61)

Furthermore, Freud worried because he believed that our conventional ethical prescriptions are foremost among the repressive elements of civilization that give life its quality of discontentedness. This is the core of the problem: instinctual life must be transformed through modification by various mechanisms that are, in essence, defensive or repressive; this is the only way we can be lifted out of the level of animal being to the level of being human. But this very process of transformation must inevitably put pressures on instinctual life, and many of these pressures must themselves be resisted. After all, we are entitled to a modicum of happiness, to some satisfaction of our instinctual desires: "A certain portion of the repressed libidinal impulses has a claim to direct satisfaction and ought to find it in life."[2]

Homosexuality can serve as a specific instance to illustrate the tension in Freud's view. On the one hand, Freud believed that part of the "proper function" of the sex instincts is to undergo a process of transformation that leads to the primacy of reproduction. Furthermore, he believed that the persistence of homosexual behavior has to do primarily with an unsatisfactory resolution of the Oedipal complex. Thus it would seem that Freud would characterize a homosexual orientation in adulthood as abnormal since it is not consistent with the proper function of the transformed instincts.

At the same time, though, Freud was loath to classify homosexuality as an illness, as is clear from the following excerpt from a letter to a mother who had inquired about psychoanalytic therapy for her son:

> I gather from your letter that your son is a homosexual. I am most impressed by the fact that you do not mention this term yourself.... May I question you why you avoid it? Homosexuality is assuredly no advantage, but it is nothing to be ashamed of, no vice, no degradation; it cannot be classified as an illness; we consider it to be a variation of the sexual function, produced by a certain arrest of sexual development.... It is a great injustice to persecute homosexuality as a crime—and a cruelty, too. (*Letters*, 423)

How does one reconcile these two views? Is homosexuality abnormal, a pathology, a pattern of behavior that any ethical system should proscribe? Or should it be welcomed as a normal variation?

Freud's answer, no doubt unsatisfying if one is looking for a simple formula, is that it is neither and both. As he indicates clearly enough in the letter, it must be allowed that adult homosexual orientation is, in the psychoanalytic view, due to a "certain arrest of sexual development." In a more detailed analysis, Freud would have discussed the processes of fixation and regression, in which, because of interpersonal factors combined with basic constitutional ones, including phylogenetic memories that precede personal experience,[3] a particular theme in sexual development becomes too strongly emphasized in adulthood. And so in this sense the homosexual is "arrested," and homosexual orientation is a flawed outcome of the transformational process of sexual development.

However, it is equally important to see that in the Freudian world *every* developmental outcome is flawed. It is impossible to imagine a case that does not entail some degree of "arrest"; the very processes of development make this inevitable. Here we begin to see how Freud's view complicates the Aristotelian concept of proper function. Freud is misleading when he says that "the purpose of life is simply the programme of the pleasure principle" (25). For it is inevitable—central to what we are—that the pleasure principle is and must be "changed into the more modest reality principle" (26). And in the process of this change, all outcomes are flawed; they are compromises between opposing forces. That the degree or magnitude of the flaw may vary is less important than the central point that all outcomes of the transformational process share this basic flaw. Fulfilling our proper function obviously entails doing so in accordance with our nature. And it is in our nature that transformation grows out of conflict.

In the social practices that are so much a part of Freud's focus in *Civilization,* prohibitions play a large role. These prohibitions, in his view, do so much harm to sexual expression that the distinction between heterosexuality and homosexuality becomes less important than the predicament we all share. Because of his assumption that all components of sexuality should, ideally, come under the umbrella of reproduction, Freud allows that "a cultural community is perfectly justified, psychologically, in starting by proscribing manifestations of the sexual life of children" (60). But he is also worried about the shape that these prohibitions take and about their effects, and here we see Freud's sympathy for all human creatures, whatever their sexual orientation:

> As regards the sexually mature individual, the choice of an object is restricted to the opposite sex, and most extra-genital satisfactions are forbidden as perversions. The requirement ... that there shall be a single kind of sexual life for everyone ... disregards the dissimilarities, whether innate or acquired, in the sexual constitution of human beings; it cuts off a fair number of them from sexual enjoyment, and so becomes the source of serious injustice. (60)

On the one hand, Freud understands that moral prescriptions and proscriptions are necessary ingredients in human life; after all, within his system the super-ego in part represents the internalization of such values that have been transmitted by parents, teachers, and others in positions of authority. Without these moral elements, the path that human life must take—the binding together by Eros of larger and larger circles of individuals—could not proceed. "Civilization," after all, "is a process in the service of Eros" (81), and it is through the transformation of instinctual energy into such products of civilization as ethical norms that this process moves forward. However, these ethical norms are also one of the biggest sources of pain and injustice in civilized life. What bothers Freud is not only or even mostly that "civilized man has exchanged a portion of his possibilities of happiness for a portion of security" (73). What he finds most troublesome is that in the process of this exchange the demands made by conventional morality are routinely too severe—they not only ask more of us than is in some sense necessary, they ask more than it is possible to deliver, given our natures.

This is the paradoxical Freud we find as we turn now to a more general discussion of his ethical views. Even as he understood the role that conventional morality played in the development of civilization, he was appalled at the cost it extracted, and he feared that this very same morality which played so necessary a role in getting us to this stage of civilized life might eventually be one source of our destruction.

THE LOVE COMMANDMENT

One purpose of Freud's discussion of the moral injunction to "love thy neighbor as thyself" seems to be simply to pave the way toward his analysis of aggression and the death instinct: for the "truth," he says, "is that men are not gentle creatures who want to be loved.... [T]hey are, on the contrary, creatures among whose instinctual endowments is to be reckoned a powerful share of aggressiveness" (68). However, as Wallwork has shown,[4] Freud's approach to the love commandment illustrates again the complexity of his ethical position. It also helps us to appreciate how Freud stands outside "the mainstream of Western moralists" (Wallwork, 199, n. 9) and how his view of human nature can illuminate ethical dilemmas.

About the love commandment, Freud asks: "Why should we do it? What good will it do us? But above all, how shall we achieve it? How can it be possible?" (66). One might think that the first two questions are easy to answer. Isn't it intuitively obvious that although we may not succeed in fulfilling the commandment entirely, it is better to try than not? That is, shouldn't we try, as the commandment asks, to love our neighbors as ourselves, even if we don't succeed? And isn't it also intuitively obvious that good will flow from such love?

There is a significant way in which Freud agreed with this sentiment. As he put it in a letter to Romaine Rolland in 1926,

> I myself have always advocated the love of mankind not out of sentimentality or idealism but for sober, economic reasons: because in the face of our instinctual drives and the world as it is I was compelled to consider this love as indispensable for the preservation of the human species as, say, technology. (*Letters*, 364)

And of course, Freud pins his hopes, however dim, on Eros: "And now it is to be expected that the other of the two 'Heavenly Powers,' eternal Eros, will make an effort to assert himself in the struggle with his equally immortal adversary" (112).

But despite the fact that Freud took very seriously the role Eros played not only in an epistemological scheme but in an ethical one as well, he concluded that the love commandment does more harm than good. In response to his first question, "Why should we [obey the commandment]?" (66), he takes a fairly narrow psychoanalytic line, arguing that for the most part, a person deserves love only if he is an object of projection or identification: "He deserves [love] if he is so like me in important ways that I can love myself in him; and he deserves it if he is so much more perfect than myself that I can love my ideal of my own self in him." But he is concerned that the love commandment, if put into action fully, would spread love around so thinly that it would lose both its meaning and its force:

> But if he is a stranger to me and if he cannot attract me by any worth of his own. . . . I should be wrong [to love him], for my love is valued by all my own people as a sign of my preferring them, and it is an injustice . . . if I put a stranger on a par with them. . . . But if I am to love him (with this universal love) merely because he, too, is an inhabitant of the earth . . . then I fear that only a small modicum of my love will fall to his share. (66)

In response to the second question—"What good will it do us?"— Freud's answer, implicitly, is "not much." The commandment is not only unreasonable; it is also unworkable. Given our nature, it is impossible to spread love around so thinly, even if we should desire to do so, because the commandment "runs so strongly counter to the original nature of man" (70).

How so? Here Freud emphasized the complex way in which Eros and the aggressive drive are alloyed. "Civilization is a process in the service of Eros," and it is the purpose of Eros "to combine single human individuals, and after that families, then races, peoples and nations, into one great unity, the unity of mankind" (81). If this were all, we might well be able to count on the love commandment to work pretty smoothly. But of course, if the human psyche was moved only by Eros, there would be no call for such a commandment.

In spite of "man's natural aggressive instinct, the hostility of each against all and all against each" (82), Freud cannot endorse the love commandment, not only because it runs counter to nature but also because "this aggressive inclination ... which forces civilization into such a high expenditure [of energy]" is, paradoxically, also responsible for some of the progress of civilization (69). Freud remarks that it is "not easy for men to give up the satisfaction of this inclination to aggression. They do not feel comfortable without it" (72). This by itself might not be sufficient grounds for the abolition of the love commandment; though aggression may be a part of our nature, one might argue for making efforts to renounce it if it had only negative effects or if it were bad in some simple, straightforward way. The difficulty is that our tendency toward aggression is a tremendous threat but also, unfortunately, an element in our progress as a species existing in civilization. This is true for both the role that aggression plays between individuals and its intrapsychic role as a prime mover of the super-ego.

"It is always possible," Freud writes, "to bind together a considerable number of people in love, so long as there are other people left over to receive the manifestations of their aggressiveness" (72). In other words, the work of Eros—binding people together in larger and larger units, a process that depends on identification—depends in a nontrivial way on the recognition of difference. This is what Freud called "the narcissism of minor differences": "[I]t [is] precisely [in] communities with adjoining territories" that feuds are most likely— "like the Spaniards and Portuguese, the North Germans and South Germans, the English and Scotch, and so on"(72). Poet and songmeister Leonard Cohen makes the same point: "Give me back the Berlin Wall / Give me Stalin and Saint Paul."[5] It is easier to rally around common goals, to recognize common purpose, when the adversary is well defined.

So even though Eros and aggression work at cross purposes, they are part of the same vector of human nature. And although Freud hoped for Eros to win out over aggression, he believed not only that it would be impossible to eradicate this part of our instinctual heritage completely but also that doing so would be undesirable. For Freud, the key is not eradication but transformation, and he is impatient at what he sees as the naiveté of the love commandment. It is not quite that "good fences make good neighbors," or even that there is something that *does* love a wall.[6] Rather—paradoxically and sadly—walls make the process of binding, the work of Eros, easier.[7] But walls in turn are impossible without the recognition of difference. And the recognition of difference, via identification (a super-ego function), relies on the aggressive instinct.

Freud's objections to the love commandment with respect to these *inter*personal and systemic problems of aggression are concerned with the impossibility, in his view, of its implementation: the commandment runs against the grain of human nature. What sense does it make, Freud asks, to enforce a commandment that simply won't work?

However, at another level the love commandment is too successful, and that is in the role it plays in amplifying the *intra*personal aggression of the super-ego on the ego. The love commandment is, in Freud's view, a central cultural manifestation of the super-ego. While the super-ego is, as a repository of a culture's norms and values, a necessary ingredient in the transformation of instinctual potential into human actuality, its effects on the human spirit are quite costly. "In the severity of its commands and prohibitions [the super-ego] troubles itself too little about the happiness of the ego. . . . Consequently we are very often obliged, for therapeutic purposes, to oppose the super-ego, and to lower its demands" (108). Here, then, Freud is arguing against the love commandment on the grounds that it works too well. While we must try to get along with our neighbors, given the often harsh role of the super-ego in our psychic economies, we must also work hard at being gentler on ourselves.[8]

Freud's attack on the love commandment has as much to do with his unhappiness about how the super-ego develops and functions as with the commandment itself. For although aggression is the enemy of civilization, it is also, as a transformation into super-ego, the enemy of the individual or the ego. The problem is that we cannot do without it. Just as the process of identification enables us, via Eros, to spread the circles of libidinal affection ever wider but also becomes the basis for the recognition of difference and enmity, the transformation of remorse and guilt into conscience is one basis for a moral approach to living but is simultaneously the seedbed for the punishing aspect of the super-ego, which only gets more powerful as more attempts are made to appease it. Because in its development the super-ego appropriates its energy more from the aggressive than from the erotic pole of the instincts, "it torments the ego ... and is on the watch for opportunities of getting it punished.... This means that virtue forfeits some of its promised reward; the docile and continent ego does not enjoy the trust of its mentor, and strives in vain, it would seem, to acquire it" (86–87).

The Place of Reason

We can see, then, that while Freud ambivalently endorses the role that the super-ego necessarily plays as the conveyor of tradition and morality, this is not where he places whatever "small hope" he possesses.[9] Because the super-ego in its development is so closely aligned with the aggressive pole of the instincts, it is just as much of a threat as the external aggression that is the original impetus for civilization. Like that external aggressive tendency, which is a necessary but nonetheless harmful ingredient in human affairs, the super-ego is simultaneously a blessing and a curse. As Freud puts it at the start of the last section of the essay, explaining why he has seemingly taken a detour away from the topic of aggression toward the sense of guilt, he wants to "represent the sense of guilt as the most important problem in the development of civilization and to show that the price we pay for our advance in civilization is a loss of happiness through the heightening of the sense of guilt" (97).

The only possible way out of this dilemma is through Reason. This may sound surprising coming from Freud. After all, "no one has done more to challenge the belief that dispassionate consideration of evidence and arguments are the predominant determinants of human conduct" (Wallwork, 229). Why does Freud put so much intellectual capital into Reason when his own picture of the human psyche seems to argue against it?

Ethics and the Place of Reason

We must remember that Freud is not saying that Reason will win the day, only that this is the only route through which we can *try* to rescue ourselves. "Reason cannot save us, nothing can; but reason can mitigate the cruelty of living" (Rieff, xxii). Still, the prescription seems to border on malpractice, given Freud's claims about the nature of the world and our place in it. If we are moved into the world by desire, and if everything we achieve is through the transformation of this desire, what role could Reason possibly play? The answer to the question lies in the fact that just as Freud's sense of sex and death was radically different from our usual sense of these concepts, so does his conceptualization of rationality differ from "the mainstream of Western moralists" (Wallwork, 199).

There is a long tradition in modern Western philosophy, cohering in a central way around Plato and Kant, that treats Reason as a function separable from desire.[10] Whereas for Freud the unconscious world of passionate desire and instinct is the source of human reality—it is where we live, so to speak—for Plato the sensual, animate world is merely an imperfect copy of the spiritual world of the Forms and therefore illusory. So "the good" in Plato's view must be sought solely in terms of this ethereal realm; he distrusted the material world. And while for Freud any prescription for good living must begin with considering what we want—although this desire must then be transformed—Kant's view "is that the will as free should not only be determined without the cooperation of sensuous desires.... [I]t should restrain all natural inclinations that might prevent the realization of law" (quoted in Wallwork, 233).

As we have already seen, much of Freud's dissatisfaction with the love commandment has to do with his commitment to the idea that the passions, at the very least, must be consulted if an ethical prescription is to be of any practical use. And Freud's conception of Reason is different from the Platonic and Kantian traditions in just this way. The task of the ego—the locus of rationality—is largely to consult the passions and then to negotiate a path for the organism through the manifold struggles of life. Freudian Reason is not isolated from human desire but rather fully connected to it.

It is also important to see why it is that while Freud is pessimistic about the ego's prospects—he is worried that we will either destroy ourselves in an orgy of aggression directed outward and orchestrated by the id or be destroyed by an "epistemologically blind, autocratic superego" (Wallwork, 222)—he is not ambivalent about it in the way he is about the id and the super-ego. The id, after all, is a "cauldron full of seething excitations" (*NIL*, 73), and it would be disastrous both individually and culturally if its contents were ever to be expressed in their raw and naked form. And the super-ego finds its version of pleasure primarily in the punishment of the ego. Thus the ego "is not even master in its own house" (*Introductory Lectures*, 285.)

We have already seen that the instincts—Eros and death—are usually alloyed together. However, we can also see in any one phenomenon the primacy of one pole or the other. Now we can go further. While the psychic apparatus as a whole is constantly producing compromise formations, both the ego and the super-ego are also subject to similar processes in their development. The development of both the ego and the super-ego are historically deep responses to the contingent particulars of our history (phylogenesis) and individual dilemmas (ontogenesis). They both develop in a fundamentally defensive and reactive way to the organism's milieu and in a way that parallels the fundamentally defensive and reactive entities they create out of their conflicts with each other, with the id, and with the world.

However, there is also a difference in the developmental paths of the ego and the super-ego, just as there is a difference in the products for which they are each chiefly responsible. The developmental path of the ego is primarily sublimatory. In his elaboration of the aphorism "Where id is, there ego shall be" (*NIL*, 80), Freud makes an analogy to the draining of the Zuider Zee for the uses of agriculture. What the ego is striving to achieve is the appropriation of the id's energies for cultural uses. Not only is the ego very pragmatic but its products—as are the products of sublimation generally—are relatively straightforward, unweird, recognizable, reasonable. Although certainly compromise formations, they do not work against the natural interests of the organism as strongly as do the products of the super-ego.

The developmental path the super-ego takes, on the other hand, is more complex. Because the super-ego is "the heir of the Oedipus complex" (*EI*, 26), its history is more one of repression than of sublimation, as are its effects; this is what so often gives the super-ego its tyrannical quality. And so while the super-ego remains the repository of values and inculcated moral codes, its usefulness as a base on which to build a workable ethic is severely compromised.

At first it may seem odd that, from within the Freudian perspective, ethics proceed from the ego rather than from the super-ego, since it is the super-ego where our moral imperatives in some sense reside. But this is really not unusual among theories of ethics. Even those—like Kant's—that most forcefully separate a moral faculty from the appetitive or sensual elements of human life still hold that the human being must reach the good or right decision through Reason.

The super-ego is ill suited for the working out of ethical rules and ethical decisions because it is in many ways like the id: demanding, passionate. Furthermore, it is the ego, not the super-ego, that best represents the interests of the entire organism. And because the ego is working, in some sense, *for* the instincts, it can stand against the abuses of a conventional morality and move toward the best of the available options for satisfaction. The super-ego, on the other hand, because of its history and because it represents the values of the society in which the individual is embedded, is working *against* the instincts and the id, even though it derives from the id and is in a real sense more instinctual than the ego. In this respect, we can see the larger battle between Eros and death reflected in the struggle between the ego and the super-ego. The ego is aligned with Eros, the super-ego with the main derivative of the death instinct, aggression.

We have already seen that implicit in Freud's approach to the ethical dilemmas posed by living is an exhortation to go easier on ourselves. His rejection of the love commandment is based in part on the insight that it is only fueling the fire of this monstrous but necessary appendage to the psychic apparatus, the super-ego. But he is not only exhorting us to be kinder with ourselves; he is also concerned that we miss much of true value in life and argues that the deflections and substitutive satisfactions we employ deserve our reprobation to the extent that they divert us from the two best possibilities: work and love.

The proposition that conventional morality does as much harm as good leads us to another way that Freud is outside the mainstream of much of Western moral philosophy. One reading of *Civilization,* which I have just emphasized in discussing the differences between the ego and the super-ego—differences, if you will, in the constituencies they serve—points up the antagonism between the individual and society, the way in which the interests of civilization run counter to the interests of the individual. But while it is true that there is tension and conflict between these interests, it is also true that, for Freud, the tension is not complete. In his view civilization is the work of Eros; it grows out of the interests of the individual. Civilization works to further the interests of the individual even as it works against them. Thus Freud does not make a dichotomous separation between the interests of the individual and the interests of society. Rather, in

> Freud's moral psychology ... the opposition of individual and society, though in certain respects incurable, is not complete—at least not in the same way that it is for those liberal philosophers who, because they view the human being as an isolated, atomistic, egoistic individual, conclude that social obligations are normally contrary to the individual's self-interest. (Wallwork, 266)

Freud's ethic is at variance with this current of Western moral philosophy because his view of human nature is similarly at variance. We are not atomistic but rather "irreducibly social. The self," for Freud, "does not exist except as constituted through the long process of psycho-social development" (Wallwork, 241). And what moves this process forward is Eros, the very same entity that moves civilization. Further, what happens as development proceeds is that egoistic and altruistic needs become very much intertwined. Eros binds people together across the full range of attachments—couples connected by sexual desire, family members by the bonds of love, citizens by a common purpose. As Wallwork has explored, implicit in the view *Civilization* presents is a rejection of the social-contract view of the liberal philosophers. Such a view might be viable if human beings were only self-interested creatures. But the Freudian person is not simple and, as a function of his inevitable developmental path, not simply self-interested. Both because we have aggressive tendencies that threaten to pull us apart and because we are moved by erotic tendencies bringing us together at multiple levels, the ethic reflected in a social-contract view is insufficient, in Freud's view, to the tasks of civilization. This view is also not sufficiently cognizant of the complex nature of human beings, who are ambivalent, conflicted, even contradictory. "Accordingly, he roots the process of civilization not only in necessity (Ananke) [which calls for some of the aspects of the social contract], but also in Eros" (Wallwork, 263).

A FREUDIAN ETHIC FOR A FREUDIAN NATURE

What, then, is the Freudian ethic?

For one thing, the ethical stance that flows from Freud's view of human nature rejects those aspects of conventional morality that either ask of human nature what it cannot deliver or reinforces those aspects of psychological functioning that are needlessly harsh and work against the individual's freedom. Indeed, enhancing the freedom of the individual to achieve insight into his or her psychological difficulties and to then take responsibility for change is the main goal of psychoanalytic therapy. And achieving this goal entails the subsidiary task of lessening the demands of the super-ego, the psychic locus of conventional morality.

But Freud's ethical view is more than simply the rejection of aspects of conventional morality. Despite his ambivalence about so much of conventional morality, he believed that "shared moral principles ... are 'necessary' to avoid the chaos that would exist if unrepressed and unsublimated instinctual impulses were given free reign" (Wallwork, 262). Furthermore, the core of his ethical view is about what we should embrace rather than about what we should resist or acquiesce to. Work and love: these are the patterns of living to which Freud gives pride of place. And they are central not because of some abstract, Kantian principle divorced from desire but rather because these two modes of activity are central to what it means to be human: "The communal life of human beings had ... a two-fold foundation: the compulsion to work ... and the power of love" (55). This leads us to an appreciation of how Freud's sense of what we ought to do is inextricably bound to his sense of what we are.

Freud hewed to an Aristotelian view of human nature in at least three senses. First, he saw human beings as having a function, though a complicated one. Second, he portrayed the movement and growth toward the realization of that function in a developmental way. Finally, it follows from this that there is something unique to human beings; we have a nature, which, although it is a product of development and history, defines who we are. Just as Aristotle argued that an individual's happiness will flow from carrying out his proper function, Freud argues that an understanding of our basic nature—in this case, the convoluted history of the transformation of the instincts—leads to certain prescriptions. Figuring importantly among these are the role that work and love can play in moving us toward the best expression of the instincts.

It is interesting for our purposes to note that Aristotle's discussion in the *Nichomachean Ethics* is actually not about our familiar notion of happiness but rather about the Greek idea of *eudaemonia*, which "is badly but inevitably translated by *happiness*. ... Aristotle's use of this word reflects the strong Greek sense that virtue and happiness cannot be entirely divorced."[11] And when Freud says that his method will allow us to "get to know the much trampled soil from which our virtues proudly spring" (*Interpretation*, 621), we see a variation of Aristotle's theme. Though Freud begins with a basic biological notion of satisfaction, virtue and satisfaction are intertwined. In the *Ethics*, Aristotle states that a person who simply seeks pleasure is slavish and cattlelike. Freud would agree, which is why the transformation of the instincts is so crucial in his view.

The basic nature of the Freudian person is very different from that of the Aristotelian one, as is the route to proper function. It is because the core of the Freudian being is a dynamic, inextricable mixture of desire and conflict that the Freudian ethic winds up being so different from the Aristotelian one in its particulars. *Eudaemonia* is an impossibility in the Freudian world, if in this *eudaemonia* there is any-thing approaching harmony. After all, to be human in the Freudian world is to be discontented, not at home.[12] But the Aristotelian and Freudian ethic nevertheless share an emphasis on the intertwining of basic nature, effective functioning, and virtue. If Eros turns out to be successful in its battle against its "equally immortal adversary" (112), it is because human beings will have managed to strike just the right balance between the satisfaction of instinctual desire, sublimation, and conformation to regulations that make social life possible.

The Freudian person is also different from the Aristotelian one in that he or she is a product of biological evolution. While Aristotle was not simply an essentialist—he acknowledged infinite gradations in the animal kingdom—he saw human beings as occupying a particular place in the "great chain of being." Although Aristotle saw the process of individual life as developmental, the idea that the place of human beings in life is a contingent rather than a necessary fact would have been foreign to him.

For Freud, on the other hand, the idea that there is a complete continuity across the animal kingdom, and that our basic nature is a contingent fact of evolution rather than given, are central to his view. Freud was sufficiently immersed in the worldview bequeathed to him by Darwin to realize that it could have been different. Like evolution-ists today, he believed that human beings are not a necessary part of the world; it just happens to have worked out that way.

Interestingly, though, in one aspect of his embrace of this evolu-tionary worldview, Freud once again showed an Aristotelian strain, this time in his embrace of Lamarckianism. What attracted Freud to the Lamarckian view was not only the idea of the inheritance of acquired characteristics, though this element is necessary for Freud's scheme of phylogenetic memory's formative role in the psychological development of the individual.[13] Freud was also attracted by the teleo-logical strain in Lamarck's theory. In the Darwinian view of evolution, there is no support for the idea of progress: life changes, but not in any particular direction. Lamarckianism, on the other hand, depicts the organism as actively tracking the world and directing its own development. In fact, this is the context for the idea of inheritance of acquired characteristics. It is within this Lamarckian context that the development of the ego and the id makes sense. "Where id was, there ego shall be" (*NIL,* 80): given a particular starting point, there is a kind of organismic striving, which, though contingent, is now proceeding in a particular direction.[14]

In his emphasis on the essential role of human desire, Freud might be taken to be making a case for a simple naturalistic ethics, to be arguing that what is good is that which satisfies the desires we happen to possess by virtue of our evolutionary history. And in giving pride of place to an ego-based reason rather than to the super-ego, he might be seen as a predecessor of late-twentieth-century pragmatism, depicting the self "as a Rube Goldberg machine that requires much tinkering, rather than as a substance with a precious essence to be discovered and cherished."[15] In seeing how both of these views are insufficiently nuanced, we will be able to reach some closure on the distinctive features of Freud's ethical view.

First, Freud has sometimes been incorrectly lumped together with those in the field of sociobiology who believe that building an ethical code is a relatively simple process of reading our neural or biological predispositions and then trying to create the conditions under which some of these predispositions can be allowed maximal expression—these are the "good ones," like reciprocal altruism—while working with or tolerating the others, such as aggression.[16] Clearly, though, if Freud can be seen as promoting a virtuous life, these virtues have a much more complex relationship to basic biological predispositions than in the sociobiological view. For Freud, the instincts are transformed, so that they operate in culture in a way that barely resembles their activity in a merely biological condition. Furthermore, we have seen that there is a major part of our instinctual heritage, one that significantly constrains and shapes our thinking, our behavior, and our imaginative life, that must nevertheless be fought: this is the death instinct, with which Eros is engaged in an eternal struggle. What this means is that for Freud, values are much more than mere preferences.

And neither can Freud be very simply fit into the mold of a pragmatist, at least not one of the Richard Rorty variety. It is true, as Rorty has put it, that Freud teaches us that the passions are not automatically suspect and that conscience is not automatically privileged. But while Freud had no tolerance for essences of the Platonic or Kantian sort, especially as commitment to these figure in punitive ethical injunctions that amplify the super-ego, he was fundamentally committed to a view about the essential nature of humankind. In this respect, he believed that psychoanalysis could serve as not a mirror of, but a window on, nature.

In neither epistemological nor ethical terms was Freud a relativist. He believed that to be human means something specific. Though we are products of a long biological process, there is nothing in the spectrum of human history that leads us to believe that our basic nature will change. Finally, we are left with the contradictoriness that is one of Freud's hallmarks: our nature is deeply formed, and yet it will be the fulfillment of a kind of Aristotelian proper function to forever work to bring one aspect of that nature to a victory over the other. In Freud's view, this is how we ought to live.

7

The Oceanic Feeling:
Freud on Faith and Love

Love of this sort is hardly distinguishable from religious feeling.
What deep and worthy love is so? whether of woman or child, or art
or music. Our caresses, our tender words, our still rapture under the
influence of autumn sunsets, or pillared vistas, or calm majestic stat-
ues, or Beethoven symphonies, all bring with them the consciousness
that they are mere waves and ripples in an unfathomable ocean of
love and beauty: our emotion in its keenest moment passes from
expression into silence; our love at its highest flood rushes beyond
its object, and loses itself in the sense of divine mystery.
                                    —George Eliot, *Adam Bede*

I cannot discover this "oceanic" feeling in myself.
                                    —Freud, *Civilization*

By his own account, Freud was a vigorously unreligious man, an atheist. *Civilization* begins with a discussion of the basis of religious sensibility, and Freud moves quickly and with confidence to the conclusion
that while he cannot deny that the oceanic feeling—"a feeling of an
indissoluble bond, of being one with the external world as a whole"—

may occur, he cannot convince himself "of the primary nature of such a feeling" (12).

Freud's arguments against the validity and worth of a religious posture are so familiar, and these times so often accommodating to worldviews that exclude a religious dimension, it may seem more appropriate to view the discussion that opens *Civilization* as merely a transition from Freud's essay published three years earlier, *The Future of an Illusion,* rather than central to our concerns here. But my rationale is that Freud's position on a faith dimension, in terms of how he saw it figuring both in his own life and in humankind generally, is important precisely because *Civilization* is, in a nontrivial way, and in addition to being many other things, also a religious text: it offers, after all, both a pronouncement about the basic conundrums of life and a prescription for how to respond to this existential predicament. From this point of view, Freud's faith posture matters. We shall see that his vigorous defense of a so-called atheistic position in fact obscures something very like a religious commitment, not to a theistic God but to Eros.

I have been using *religion* and *faith* interchangeably. In part, this is because Freud himself failed to distinguish between them. In *The Future of an Illusion,* in which he made his most sustained attack against religion, Freud was not only attacking its institutional and credal aspects but also arguing that religious sensibility is an infantile psychological state of being that should be superseded by reason. Freud's critique of religion would not have been as influential in theological circles as it has if he had restricted himself to its institutional and credal dimensions. He is often seen as one of the authors of postmodern alienation and even nihilism, because his arguments not only complicated and unsettled our relationship to institutional religious activity but called into question the value of any faith posture whatsoever.

In our day, and partly by his own doing, this question of Freud's avowed incapacity for religious sensibility may seem quaint, irrelevant to our concerns. Wilfred Cantwell Smith argues that it is impossible for any individual to be totally without faith,[1] and this point of view is not at all exceptional within the context of modern liberal theology.

At the heart of Paul Tillich's idea of faith as ultimate concern, for example, is the claim that faith may be found in many different places and is certainly not restricted to conventional theism.[2] Since Freud's attitude toward his "god, *Logos,*"[3] has often been described as worshipful, might we simply say that Freud found his ultimate concern in science or psychoanalysis and leave it at that?

The question cannot be left in such a facile way, for two related reasons. First, to a significant degree, modern liberal theology has already absorbed the critique of conventional religious belief mounted by Feuerbach, Freud, Marx, and Nietzsche. But what has been the cost of this response? If faith is translated into, some would say reduced to, ultimate concern, is this a kind of faith worth keeping? What are its commitments? As Alasdair MacIntyre has argued, if faith in God is replaced by "belief in belief,"[4] then something essential has been lost, and "theists are offering atheists less and less in which to disbelieve" (MacIntyre, 24).

Second, Freud's avowed atheism is coupled to a commitment to Eros that has the characteristics of a religious posture or faith stance and that is more filled with content—belief in something rather than belief in belief—than the more inclusive definitions of religion and faith that were developed partly as a response to his own attacks. Paradoxically, Freud's commitment to Eros has all of the characteristics of a bona fide religious commitment to a theistic entity: Eros is real but unseen, though its evidence is everywhere; it is part of our nature but also somehow apart from it; it is, via sublimation, the only source of redemption; finally, to the degree that human beings successfully embrace Eros as a real force in the world (Lear, 1990), they will be able to find what is of real value in life (that is, a Freudian notion of the sacred) and steer clear of the destructive (the profane).

Let us turn, then, to Freud's avowed incapacity to discover within himself the oceanic feeling, what Romaine Rolland described to him as "a sensation of 'eternity,' a feeling of something limitless, unbounded." According to Freud's account, Rolland believed that "one may ... call oneself religious on the ground of this oceanic feeling alone, even if one rejects every belief and every illusion" (11).

The Oceanic Feeling: Freud on Faith and Love

Freud, of course, did reject everything he viewed as illusion, and for him religion and illusion were one and the same. In his view, religion was a primitive and infantile way of attempting to understand the world, one that must be left behind in favor of reason. Freud's hostility toward institutional religion can be readily understood in the context of two significant historical dimensions. First, as many students of his life and work have pointed out, Freud was a son of the Enlightenment. As we have already seen, Freud was descended from a line of scientists who were eager to remove all vestiges of vitalism and mysticism from science and to understand all physical and biological phenomena in materialistic terms. Explanations of natural (including psychological) phenomena that invoked any sort of deity were, in this context, to be shunned. That in the late twentieth century organized religion and science can seem in many instances to coexist peacefully is due in part to the long process of secularization that began before Freud but that was at full throttle during the years he matured. An adherence to the claim that religion is more likely to be a source of illusion than of insight is understandable in this context.

Second, the Vienna in which Freud spent virtually his whole life was both anti-Semitic and very Catholic. Even if Freud had not been exposed to the rituals of the Catholic church by his nursemaid,[5] the association between church practice and the sense of persecution he felt as a Jew might have been sufficient to turn him against religious practice.

So we can understand how, if Freud were a less insightful man, he might lump together matters of faith with institutional church practices and go on his merry (or dour) secular way. However, a close look at his central claims and assumptions about the function of human life reveals something nearly, if not totally, incompatible with his position on faith and the oceanic feeling. As Lear (1990) has pointed out, in giving a central role to Eros in human life, Freud was arguing that love is a force in the world. That such a force could not be explored or dissected with the usual scientific methods and tools did not, for Freud, make Eros any less real; rather, the reality of Eros as an inescapable fact of life seemed to be validated by the new tools psychoanalysis offered.

Freud's comments on the oceanic feeling are astounding even when read simply against the backdrop of his theory of the psyche, forgetting for the moment his obtuseness about religious questions. After telling his reader that he cannot discover the oceanic feeling in himself, Freud adds, "It is not easy to deal scientifically with feelings" (11). This sounds very odd coming from the man who is most associated with the scientific study of emotional life.

But this is only the beginning. What Rolland seems to have in mind, Freud says, "is a feeling of an indissoluble bond, of being one with the external world as a whole" (12). In light of Freud's concept of instinct, in which the instinct is held to be not the bodily impulse itself but rather its psychical representative, "a sort of delegate sent into the psyche by the soma" (Laplanche and Pontalis, 215), his response to Rolland's description is quite curious:

> The idea of men's receiving an intimation of their connection with the world around them through an immediate feeling which is from the outset directed to that purpose sounds so strange and fits in so badly with the fabric of our psychology that one is justified in attempting to discover a psycho-analytic—that is, a genetic—explanation of such a feeling. (12)

We can understand Freud's objection to the idea that this oceanic feeling is "from the outset directed to that purpose," but Freud seems to have read this into Rolland's description without warrant. It is certainly possible to entertain the concept of the oceanic feeling without assuming that it is purposeful. After all, Rolland, spoke of the oceanic feeling as "a purely subjective fact " (11).

More puzzling is Freud's statement that the oceanic feeling "fits in so badly with our psychology." It is this claim that moves Freud into his own genetic explanation. In the process, he recapitulates in the remainder of this section of the essay many of the points about the development of the psyche from the psychoanalytic point of view.

What is striking about this recapitulation is how well, rather than how poorly, Freud's depiction can be integrated with Rolland's. "Normally," Freud says, "there is nothing of which we are more certain than the feeling of our self, of our own ego. But such an appearance is deceptive.... [T]he ego is continued inwards, without any sharp delimitation, into an unconscious mental entity which we designate as the id" (12). In other words, it is because of the essential continuity of id and ego that the self can receive just the sort of intimation about its connectedness to the natural world that would be impossible if there were, to use a physicalist metaphor of which Freud might have approved, a relatively impermeable barrier between id and ego. But this is not the case: in Freud's view, the ego appropriates all of its energy from the id, and there is no way to say sensibly where one ends and the other begins. The ego is constantly receiving intimations about all sorts of connections to a deeper world—to the body, to nature, and, important for Freud's theory, to its own phylogenetic and ontogenetic history (including the instinctual content of Oedipal inheritance, which functions in the Freudian myth in a way that is parallel to the biblical story of the Fall). So it does not seem that the oceanic feeling fits in very badly at all with "the fabric" of Freud's psychology. What is Freud's problem here?

At least part of the difficulty is that he now makes an assumption about "where" the source of the oceanic feeling would have to reside. Whereas the ego is open on the inside, that is, toward the id, "towards the outside ... the ego seems to maintain clear and sharp lines of demarcation" (13). Freud's assumption, again most curious, is that any validating source for the oceanic feeling would have to come from outside the organism, outside the ego. In making this assumption, Freud betrays his conception about the relationship between the holy, in Rudolf Otto's sense of "the numinous," and the mundane. While such an assumption is to be expected on the basis of the positivist and materialist context in which Freud saw himself, it nevertheless needs to be examined further, since so much of Freud's theory seems to transcend these materialist, positivist roots. In the Freudian world, after all, "the unconscious is the true psychical reality" (*Interpretation*, 613); it is difficult to see why Freud would, in the context of religious experience, confer validity only on sources outside the organism.

Freud says that the ego "*seems* to maintain clear and sharp lines of demarcation," but then qualifies this statement in a rather significant way. He says that "at the height of being in love the boundary between ego and object threatens to melt away. *Against all evidence of his senses,* a man who is in love declares that 'I' and 'you' are one, and is prepared to behave as if it were a fact" (13; my emphasis). In addition, there are many instances of abnormal function "in which the boundary lines between the ego and the external world become uncertain or in which they are actually drawn incorrectly. . . . Thus, even the feeling of our own ego is subject to disturbances and the boundaries of the ego are not constant"(13). When the id informs the ego, as it always does, the boundaries between the two are fluid: they meld into each other, so that the bottom sources on which the ego relies, by virtue of their long and deep histories, are impossible to separate neatly from the ego itself. As we have already seen, Freud emphasized the difficulty of making simple distinctions between the normal and the pathological. The realm of the id is dark and deep, and out of its dynamic interaction with the ego almost anything may emerge. And with respect to these products of the id, a distinction as to their validity or invalidity is quite beside the point. And while Freud seems to have more confidence about the demarcation between the ego and the outside world, he is forced to concede that this boundary too is necessarily more fluid than one might at first think. Not only does it blur, but something like feelings of oneness—indeed, of indissoluble bonds—will "normally" appear.

In what way, then, can the idea of the oceanic feeling be said to "fit so badly" with the psychoanalytic view? Only in the sense that, for Freud, accepting the validity of the oceanic feeling would mean accepting in some kind of positivistic way a specific religious claim: that there is some kind of palpable God "out there" that is responsible for this feeling in us whenever it occurs. Freud's hardheadedness about what a religious orientation could consist of—about, if you will, the varieties of religious experience—blindsided him to seeing what seems clear from his own picture of the psyche, namely that "where" a perception comes from is neither the only nor a very important factor in considering its validity. What we take in even from those aspects of the world that we can most confidently call "the outside" is perceived through a process that necessarily involves the inner world as well. Ironically, the sharp distinction between inner and outer that

Freud wants to hold on to so tenaciously in his discussion of religion is the very distinction that his own life's work did so much to undermine. Indeed, it was through his own work at dissolving this boundary that his commitment to Eros was able to flourish.

But Freud's hostility toward religious faith is so indiscriminate that it closes him off to the possibility that any sort of faith posture might function productively in human life. True, he allows that, as one of the protections against human suffering, religion as he understands and delimits it may spare "many people an individual neurosis." He is quick to add, however, that it offers "hardly anything more." The person of religious faith "is admitting that all that is left to him as a last possible consolation and source of pleasure in his suffering is an unconditional submission. And if he is prepared for that, he could probably have spared himself the *détour* he has made" (36).

We are thus left with the impression that any rapprochement between Freud's psychoanalytic view and even a very broad notion of religious sensibility is impossible. Except, that is, for Eros. Freud's commitment to the reality and power of Eros forces us to take a closer look both at his claim that he could not identify the oceanic feeling within himself and his summary dismissal of the validity of this state, which seems after all to fit in with the fabric of his psychology rather well, certainly better than he thought.

To explore this connection between faith and Eros, let us consider George Eliot's claim that deep and worthy love is essentially indistinguishable from religious feeling. If something like Rolland's oceanic feeling is common to both love and religious sentiment, which Eliot suggests and which follows directly from a consideration of Freud's theory of sexuality and object-choice, then Freud's claims *against* religious sensibility are contradicted by his claims *for* the place of love in psychoanalytic transactions. After all, as Freud put it in a letter to Jung, psychoanalysis "is essentially a cure through love" (quoted in Gay 1988, 301).

The comparison of Freud and Eliot is not arbitrary: not only did they share, in many respects, a common intellectual, philosophical, and scientific milieu; the parallels in their views on love and moral commitment are also quite striking. The Darwinian revolution is important in understanding the thinking of both, and evolutionary ideas figure prominently in Eliot's fiction just as they do in Freud's work. Eliot's work at the *Westminster Review* brought her into intimate contact with Darwin's ideas. She also knew Herbert Spencer well and together with George Henry Lewes closely followed the emergence of the "development theory," as evolutionary ideas were then collectively referred to; she read *The Origin of Species* immediately upon its publication. Although Eliot's *Middlemarch*, in its own way another story of civilization and its discontents, is too grand, complex, and startling a book to be reduced to any one influence, the organizing idea of the "web of affinities" depends on analogies to and metaphors of biological life.[6]

In addition, both Freud and Eliot rejected conventional theism and institutional religion, but both insisted nevertheless on the importance of establishing a moral footing in this new and godless world. In Eliot's view, "God was 'inconceivable,' immortality 'unbelievable,' but duty nonetheless 'peremptory and absolute.' "[7] Though taking very different approaches, they were both what MacIntyre has called self-conscious atheists. That is, they were "systematically [asking] the questions to which traditional theism gives answers" (MacIntyre, 15).

Freud hardly seems to have struggled with theism. Although he was impressed with the arguments for the existence of God Brentano offered him during his university years, he proclaimed his atheism publicly and loudly and seemed confident and unconflicted about his position.[8]

On the other hand, Eliot's move away from theism was filled with personal struggle. Early in her life, she was thrown into conflict by scientific works such as Lyell's *Principles of Geology*, which undermined the claim that biblical accounts offered literal truth. In 1844, at 25 years of age, Eliot took over the translation of George Friedrich Strauss's *Das Leben Jesu*. "Strauss came at the end of a line of German theological critics who had . . . demolished the supernatural element in Christianity." In 1853, Eliot began her translation of Feuerbach's *Essence of Christianity*, the same text that so influenced Freud. This immersion in biblical criticism and a radically revisionary theology, woven together with her continuing reading in the natural sciences, moved Eliot away from any conventional theism. While she seems to have accomplished this move with intellectual confidence, she did not do it happily, for she still valued "the symbolic importance of ... Christian teaching, indeed of all religions based on notions of self-sacrifice, of spiritual community, of supporting love" (Uglow, 38–39).[9]

Although the paths of intellectual development for Freud and Eliot differ in their particulars, their philosophical commitments overlap substantially. In addition to their common outlook on science and the degree to which an understanding of human life can be enriched by an appreciation of its embeddedness in the rest of nature, Eliot and Freud also agreed that the urges, the wishes, of emotional life must be renounced to further the work of civilization.

A pervasive theme in Eliot's fiction is the connection between the bonds that are established between people and the commitments that these bonds create, a theme highly reminiscent of the binding work of Eros in *Civilization*. She believed that meeting these responsibilities can bring as profound a satisfaction as is to be found.[10] Love, for Eliot, is a fundamental source of authority, just as it is for Freud, who put it this way in *Three Essays:*

> The subject becomes, as it were, intellectually infatuated ... by the mental achievements and perfections of the sexual object and he submits to the latter's judgements with credulity. Thus the credulity of love becomes an important, if not the most fundamental, source of *authority*. (150; italics in original)

Although I have taken this remark out of the context of a somewhat technical discussion about the overvaluation of sexual objects, the general point still stands: Eros is in the end for Freud the only justification for the endeavors we undertake, for the myriad relationships we seek to establish.

Because of these similarities between Freud and Eliot, the differences between them are helpful in exploring Freud's problem with the oceanic feeling. To help articulate these differences, I want to turn to a more contemporary figure, Walker Percy.[11] In *Lost in the Cosmos,* as in much of his fiction, one of Percy's central concerns is his claim that we live in a scientific and postreligious world, in many respects the same world that Freud applauded and helped to usher in and that Eliot saw the necessity of adjusting to. The fundamental existential problem of such an age, in Percy's view, is that it denies us the possibility of traditional, that is to say, religious, modes of placing or naming the self in relation to the rest of the cosmos. In the absence of such religious modes of placement, one way of attempting to step outside our predicament is through what Percy calls transcendence, and there are two ways to attempt such transcendence: science and art.

Both Freud and Eliot would have assented to Percy's central claim, that they were living in a scientific and postreligious age and, in their different ways, were glad of the fact. Freud was certainly the less ambivalent of the two, enthusiastically propounding the virtues of the scientific Weltanschauung. But Eliot, with just as much intensity, if more personal struggle, was exploring the consequences of living in a world that is thoroughly natural, a world that cannot, as her study of biblical criticism and theology had taught her, profitably be seen in a theistic way.

For Percy, of the two routes to transcendence available in the modern age, science is distinctly the lesser. In his view this is so because the scientist insists that he can know the peculiar predicament of the self by using the same methodological framework he uses to understand all other phenomena. In other words, the scientist does not see the self as anything special. And it should be noted that Freud—as scientist—is one of Percy's frequent targets.

The artist in our postreligious, scientific age, on the other hand, is in a better position because he is coping with the central existential dilemma posed by the unavailability of traditional modes of placement: the unspeakability of the self. In Percy's view, the artist is at least trying to deal with the problem posed by modern existence, while the scientist is not and, as long as he restricts himself to the usual methods and approaches, cannot.

Percy's framework helps us understand an important difference between Freud and Eliot. It is not so simple as to say that Freud is an exemplar of the scientist, Eliot an exemplar of the artist. I think Percy is too hard on Freud, for Freud is not your typical scientist. Notice the difference between Percy's and Lear's views of Freud. Percy takes

Freud at his word when he says that he is using the usual scientific tools and concludes that Freud must therefore necessarily fail to understand our existential predicament. On the other hand, essential to Lear's attempt to position Freud as importantly eccentric to science in the usual sense is his claim that along with Freud's commitment to Eros came his development of a "science of subjectivity"—changing the method precisely because of the peculiar nature of the subject. Freud insists too much that he is simply doing science; the evidence of his own life—of his friendship, his commitments—and of his work puts the lie to his claim. But for all that, Freud wants to believe that science can serve us, that it can—indeed, it should and must—fully supplant traditional, i.e., religious modes of placement.

It may finally be true, as Freud of all people said, that we cannot deal scientifically with our deepest emotional life, and for the kinds of reasons that Percy develops in *Lost in the Cosmos:* the self, and the predicament of the self in a world, are qualitatively different phenomena from the rest of the events in the cosmos. The exploration of the predicament of the self therefore calls for methods that are also qualitatively different. The irony is that it was Freud who gave us these very methods: his own work and emerging vision of the world challenged the claims emanating from a more narrow, positivistic science he does seem to have worshipped.

And George Eliot is not your typical artist. Only after absorbing the most revolutionary and tradition-wrecking scientific developments of her day did she turn to fiction, creating a body of work in which she struggled with how to live in the modern world. She would no doubt have agreed with Freud that Percy described the modern world correctly. But she does not have Freud's unambiguous, enthusiastic commitment to this worldview; to a large degree, she wishes it were otherwise.[12]

Eliot continued to look for ways in which human beings might be able to find redemption, even as she realized that such redemption would not resemble anything offered by an institutional religion that demanded adherence to creed. Implicit in this stance was an openness to new ways of construing the world, even if some options—theism importantly among them—were ruled out. Part and parcel of this openness was an uncertainty coupled to a sense of wonder. Freud, on the other hand, seems quite sure about the way the world is. On ultimate questions, he is like Tolstoy's stereotypic German in *War and Peace* whose "self-assurance is the worst of all, more inflexible and repellent than any other, because he imagines that he knows the truth, science, which is his own invention, but which for him is absolute truth."[13]

But for all of these differences, the similarities of Freud's and Eliot's commitments run very deep. In *Civilization,* Freud argues for the satisfactions of dutiful work. Eliot makes much the same case in *Middlemarch.* Although his strong ambition for public recognition surely marks Freud as a different character from Dorothea Brooke, the central protagonist in *Middlemarch,* he nevertheless would have agreed with the narrator, in her closing view of Dorothea, about the value of this dutiful work done in anonymity:

> The effect of her being on those around her was incalculably dif-
> fusive, for the growing good of the world is partly dependent on
> unhistoric acts, and that things are not so ill with you and me as
> they might have been is half owing to the number who lived faith-
> fully a hidden life and rest in unvisited tombs.[14]

In *Civilization,* after describing isolation as one path to a modicum of temporary happiness, Freud stresses that "there is, indeed, another and a better path: that of becoming a member of the human community.... Then one is working with all for the good of all" (27). Here again he reminds us of Dorothea, always struggling but deciding finally to continue what can be described as an erotic commitment to the world:

> [S]he felt the largeness of the world and the manifold wakings of
> men to labour and endurance. She was a part of that involuntary,
> palpitating life and she could neither look out on it from her lux-
> urious shelter as a mere spectator nor hide her eyes in selfish
> complaining. (Eliot, 765)

In the end, Freud's strident claims about the impotence of a religious sensibility broadly construed and about his inability to discover the oceanic feeling within himself contradict not only his personal life and work but also the central product of that life and work, his story of the natural history of the self.

In the natural history of the self according to Freud, we are all lost in this cosmos. By virtue of being alive, we have suffered a fundamental disconnection,[15] and because of this all of our activities are motivated by the desire to reestablish that connection. And our knowledge—though unconscious—of this fundamental disconnection is also, in Freud's scheme, causally related to the oceanic feeling, which he described as a sense of boundarilessness between ego and object. So if we assume that the oceanic feeling is the "true source of religious sentiment," as Romaine Rolland evidently suggested to Freud, then Freud must allow that it exists within himself and indeed that it must exist in all of us.

Of course, Freud's explanation of the origin of religious sentiment does not employ the concept of the oceanic feeling. Rather, he characterizes religious feeling as infantile because of its connection, in his scheme, to the Oedipal scenario of the killing of the father, followed by identification and guilt. However, this scenario, which Freud took so literally as a historical occurrence, is merely the event that propels us on a search, both as a species and as individuals, to recover what we have lost.

I am not the first to suggest that the Oedipal story plays the same functional role in the Freudian myth as the story of Eden plays in the biblical one. In either case, this theme of lost connection, of reestablishing a prior state of affairs, is central. And this resemblance between the two myths can remind us about the religious content of Freud's commitment to Eros. While Freud certainly held that conventional theistic belief was infantile in nature, what he could not see was that his commitment to Eros was conventionally religious in many respects.

Let us return to Eliot's claim that deep love and religious feeling are "hardly distinguishable." Freud must assent to this, it seems to me, and within the framework of the oceanic feeling can no more object to religious feeling than to deep love, which he values so highly both as a goal and an ingredient in the life well lived. What Freud failed to see is that atheism, beyond its narrow definition-by-contrast to theism, implies a kind of radical disconnection from which he would certainly withhold his approval. For it seems clear enough that Freud really did possess the very kind of religious sensibility he denied so vigorously.

What Eliot helps us to see is that moving away from a particular dogmatic claim need not have anything to do with one's basic religious stance. In regard to Freud, this means that he was really more religious than he was able to articulate, and this has to do in part with his confusion between dogma and faith. The remainder of his failure to see the religious aspect of his own life and work has to do with his reasonable enough assumption that when one is talking about religion, one is talking about theism. It is difficult to know what one would do with an Eros-ology that might replace theology. But on the other hand, such an Eros-ology is certainly more specific and, if handled well, perhaps more valuable, than mere "belief in belief."[16]

I am not recommending some sort of orgiastic religion over a conventional, theistic one. All I want to suggest is that Freud's commitment to Eros has some of the basic ingredients of a bona fide religious commitment that I listed earlier in this chapter. Does this exonerate Freud from the charge of being one of the authors of the nihilism of our age? No, since he has without doubt been a contributor; as is said so often these days, acts have consequences. It does seem clear, though, that Freud was no nihilist himself, even if he did not recognize that his commitment to Eros both transcended the narrow positivism he used to attack theism and, furthermore, was much like that theism.

8

Women, Femininity, and the Import of Ideology

The status of women is held in the heart and the head as well as the home: oppression has not been trivial or historically transitory—to maintain itself so effectively it courses through the mental and emotional bloodstream.... [O]nce again we need pessimism of the intellect, optimism of the will.

—Juliet Mitchell, *Psychoanalysis and Feminism*

dreaming of orgies in Vegas or Cannes
He preens and strikes poses Olympian
While she shoulders the cross
And lets him play boss
His nurse and long-suffering Samaritan
He brags about knocking the world on its ass
But oh, when the shit hits the fan
She'll bail him out, she's the one with the clout
Only she knows how humankind ever began
What does a woman see in a man?

—Jimmy Webb, "What Does a Woman See in a Man?"

Freud's statements about women, his claims about their inferior moral and intellectual status, are notorious even within the context of a generally controversial theory of human nature. In *Civilization,* he tells us that

> women soon come into opposition to civilization and display their retarding and restraining influences.... The work of civilization has become increasingly the business of men, it confronts them with ever more difficult tasks and compels them to carry out instinctual sublimations of which women are little capable. (59)

But even this statement seems tame when compared to others Freud made at different points in his life. For example:

> [With respect to polymorphous perversity] children behave in the same kind of way as an average uncultivated woman.... [C]onsidering the immense number of women who are prostitutes or who must be supposed to have an aptitude for prostitution ... it becomes impossible not to recognize that this same disposition to perversions of every kind is a general and fundamental human characteristic. (*Three Essays,* 57)

And infamously:

> To those of you who are women ... you are yourselves the problem.... The fact that women must be regarded as having little sense of justice is no doubt related to the predominance of envy in their mental life; for the demand for justice is a modification of envy and lays down the condition subject to which one can put envy aside. We also regard women as weaker in their social interests and as having less capacity for sublimating their instincts than men.... A man of about thirty strikes us as a youthful, somewhat unformed individual, who we expect to make powerful use of the possibilities for development opened up to him by analysis. A woman of the same age, however, often frightens us by her psychical rigidity and unchangeablity. Her libido has taken up final positions and seems incapable of exchanging them for others. There are no paths open to further development; it is as though the whole process had already run its course ... as though,

indeed, the difficult development to femininity had exhausted the possibilities of the person concerned. (*NIL,* 113, 134–35)

Freud was aware of the opposition to his work by feminist writers of his day: "We must not allow ourselves to be deflected … by the denials of the feminists, who are anxious to force us to regard the two sexes as completely equal in position and worth."[1] Within the psycho-analytic tradition and more or less contemporaneous with Freud, these feminist critics included analysts Clara Thompson and Karen Horney, who strove to illuminate from within the home camp the shortcomings of Freud's hypotheses. The middle decades of the twentieth century saw the emergence, after his death, of the "second wave" of feminism. While all of the leaders of this movement—including Simone de Beauvoir, Betty Friedan, Germain Greer, Shulamith Firestone, and Kate Millett[2]—were concerned with much more than Freud and psychoanalysis, they all agreed, though from different perspectives and with different emphases, that Freud's deficiencies as a theorist vastly outweighed his merits and argued for moving into the future without him.

It seems hard to avoid the fact that Freud held a negative view of women. While it may be difficult to prove the global charge that "Freud built a theoretical structure permeated with the residue of his fears and negativity toward women," it seems fair enough to say that he carried out his work throughout his life "separated from the experience of women's lives."[3] The excerpts that opened this chapter support the claim that Freud was far from neutral about women and often seemed woefully embedded in patriarchy and misogyny.

It may seem odd, then, that over the past 25 years there has developed a broad current of feminist thought that, while still scornful of Freud's claims about women's intellectual and moral status, nevertheless holds that the feminist agenda will be difficult to move forward without a Freudian perspective. Nancy Chodorow, for example, rejects Freud's central claims about Oedipal dynamics and takes him to task for his patriarchal and misogynistic attitude but at the same time believes that "psychoanalytic theory remains the most convincing, coherent theory of personality development available for an understanding of fundamental aspects of the psychology of women in our society, in spite of its biases" (Chodorow 1978, 142). Jane Flax takes a similar position, arguing that "for all its shortcomings psychoanalysis presents the best and most promising theories [of the development of] a self that is simultaneously embodied, social, 'fictional,' and real."[4] Juliet Mitchell goes so far as to suggest that "a rejection of psychoanalysis and of Freud's thought is fatal for feminism" (quoted in Gardiner, 437).

What joins these contemporary feminists together is the belief that patriarchy and its resulting inequality and oppression are deeply imbedded not in our biological natures but in our psychological and cultural ones. Consequently, to make sense of this patriarchy and oppression, one needs a framework that makes an appropriately parallel core assumption about how attitudes and ways of being become so embedded in the "mental and emotional bloodstream." And Freudianism appears to offer such a framework.

We shall see in this chapter, first of all, that Freud's statements about the intellectual and moral inferiority of women are not just offhand remarks. These conclusions flow from his theory, even as that theory reinforces the cultural prejudices of Freud's day. However, we shall also see that a thorough understanding of this theory in fact yields a very different view of "the feminine" than that which comes from looking only at Freud's notorious comments about women. Finally, the embrace of Freudianism coupled with a rejection of Freud's specific claims about the status of women by a broad current of contemporary feminism makes good sense.

To appreciate why contemporary feminist theorists often find Freud useful, we must first see how he arrived at his conclusions about the inferiority of women. For Freud, the essential differences in the psychology of men and women can be traced back to the different fate of the Oedipus complex in boys and girls.[5] At the level of individual development, the story goes in this way.

Every child's first object of love is the mother: "a child sucking at his mother's breast has become the prototype of every relation of love" (*Three Essays,* 222). In the case of little boys, the child maintains this attachment and comes to view the father as a rival. The boy also fears that he will lose his genitals, as it appears to him has already happened to little girls. But because the boy's fear and hostility toward the father are intermixed with love, he is able to partly transform these destructive emotions into a grudging kind of admiration and eventually into an identification with the ways of the father. As this identification develops, the boy is able to resolve his attachment to his mother and go on to seek out other objects of attachment in his maturity, using the model of the father as a path. In this way, it is the boy's fear of castration that leads him eventually beyond the Oedipal complex:

> *in boys the Oedipus complex is destroyed by the castration complex.* ... [T]he complex is not simply repressed, it is literally smashed to pieces by the shock of threatened castration. Its libidinal cathexes are abandoned, desexualized, and in part sublimated; its objects are incorporated into the ego, where they form the nucleus of the super-ego and give that new structure its characteristic qualities. In normal, or, it is better to say, in ideal cases, the Oedipus complex exists no longer, even in the unconscious; the super-ego has become its heir. ("Consequences," 256–57; italics in original)

In girls, the ontogenetic story differs in important ways. Like boys, a girl's first object of desire is her mother. However, girls face a task in the course of psychosexual development that boys do not: if they are to successfully negotiate the vicissitudes of early and adolescent life (meaning, in this case, moving toward objects of the opposite sex and establishing a heterosexual relationship),[6] they must make a switch; unlike boys, they cannot attach to objects that are modeled in some way on the mother but must instead turn to objects that resemble the father. The girl's path toward the father as an object of affection, in Freud's view, is prepared by the awareness of her own deficiency. Just as the boy's hostility for the father is intermixed with love and admiration, the girl's love for her mother is complicated by hostility and blame. Once the little girl notices that she, like her mother, is without a penis, she in good part transfers her affections to the father, wanting what he has. Eventually, Freud claims, the girl child will draw an equivalence between a penis and a baby, and the attraction to the father will be complete. Thus,

> *in girls [the Oedipus complex] is made possible and led up to by
> the castration complex.* ... [T]he motive for the demolition of the
> Oedipus complex is lacking. Castration has already had its effect,
> which was to force the child into the situation of the Oedipus
> complex. Thus the Oedipus complex escapes the fate which it
> meets with in boys: it may be slowly abandoned or dealt with by
> repression, or its effects may persist far into women's normal
> mental life. ("Consequences," 256–57; italics in original)

In the development of women, then, there is no clearly demarcated and well-endowed super-ego because its predecessor, the Oedipus complex, has never clearly met with its demise, been "smashed to pieces," as it has in boys.

Freud, then, is linking together two claims, about penis envy and about a stunted level of moral development. What is the basis for this apparently bizarre concatenation? First, Freud argues that the evidence for the ontogenetic story falls out of his clinical experience, that the theme of penis envy is revealed in the analysis of women's dreams, for example. Second, his thinking here is constrained again by the idea that ontogeny recapitulates phylogeny.[7] In emphasizing the relationship between what transpires at the ontogenetic level and what has been both inherited and freshly acquired from the phylogenetic level, Freud would like us to believe that the psychological, moral, and intellectual differences he sees between men and women are "an intelligible consequence" not only "of the anatomical distinction between their genitals" but also of the "psychical situation" involved in this distinction ("Consequences," 257). This "psychical situation," a core component of our ancestral memory, has mostly to do with Freud's myth about the beginnings of civilization.

In his telling, the beginnings of civilization are found in the killing of the father by the primal horde of brothers.[8] These brothers are motivated by the father's authoritarian and brutal ways, which include the threat of castration and a monopoly on sexual resources. After having acted on these rivalrous feelings toward the father, however, the brothers feel guilt and remorse over their act. Out of this guilt and remorse come identification with the ways of the father, a totemic identification and idealization, and the beginnings of culture.

What is important to note here is the formal similarity between these events, which Freud believed were actually played out at the phylogenetic level, and the relationships he believed existed between male child and father at the ontogenetic level. The male child views the father as a rival not only, perhaps not even mostly, because of his own experience. The male child is constrained here by a central piece of phylogenetic inheritance: "[W]hat is at bottom inherited is nevertheless freshly acquired in the development of the individual" (*Introductory Lectures*, 354–55). As we saw in chapter 6, Freud believed that human beings had a particular kind of nature, which includes in a central way the Oedipal beginnings of human culture and human affectional relationships.

What is missing in this primal scenario is any role for women; it is not the brothers and sisters that band together but the brothers alone. Thus it is only in these developing men that we see the transformation of guilt and remorse into identification and idealization. But identification and idealization, after all, are the beginnings of the super-ego, what will become in the human psyche both the repository of cultural values and the impetus to sublimation in the form of intellectual and moral work. Men, Freud believed, inherit this phylogenetic precipitate directly, whereas women acquire it only through what he referred to fuzzily as "cross-inheritance" ("Consequences," 258).

But how does the phenomenon of penis envy figure in this picture? On what basis does Freud connect a stunted morality and this specific form of envy? As many commentators have suggested, Freud would have stood on somewhat less controversial ground if he had treated the theme of penis envy in a less literal and more metaphorical sense, with the penis symbolizing male power.

Certainly we must allow that Freud's views here are partly the reflection of what Chodorow has called patriarchal distortions. This cannot be forgotten or minimized. But while keeping this in mind, and for all its apparent absurdity, there are two bases within Freud's theory for his claim about the centrality of actual penis envy, as opposed to a symbolic or even merely metaphoric form, in the moral and intellectual lives of women.

First, there is the claim that the castration complex is the ontogenetic expression of the Oedipal dynamic. Because in our phylogenetic history the primal brothers feared castration by the primal father, this constellation of content influences unconscious mental life in the current generation. While boys are not motivated originally by envy but by fear, little girls, in Freud's view, operate with the assumption that they actually have been castrated; it is too late for fear, and envy is the more appropriate emotional response. And both boys' fear and girls' envy are directed specifically and concretely at the genitals.

The second reason for Freud's specific emphasis on the genitals is less directly related to this primal Oedipal theme than to his ideas about the nature of libido and to his broader conceptualization of sexuality. Because, as we saw in chapter 5, Freud conceptualized sexuality at the psychological level as being concerned with the finding of sexual objects, he took libido to be essentially masculine in nature. That is, he equated the active mode with masculinity, and because he viewed libido as an active energy, indeed as a primary mover of human action, libido could only be masculine.[9] Once this equation is made, it is but a short step to conceptualize the penis as the organ of seeking and activity, the vagina the organ of receptivity and passivity.

While Freud's tacit equation of the penis with the active mode reflects much stereotypical thinking about sexuality, the point must be made that this is the kind of assumption that still figures heavily today in our struggles to conceptualize sexuality. The idea that at the base of masculinity is a predisposition toward activity, and at the base of femininity a predisposition toward passivity or receptivity, finds wide currency, even if these equations may beg the question of to what extent the very concepts of masculinity and femininity are useful.

We have seen that it is possible to find a logic from within Freud's theory that leads to his conclusions about the moral and intellectual inferiority of women, and the connection of this double inferiority to core Freudian issues of sexuality. But what does this show? If Freud's conjectures about the prehistoric beginnings of culture and his assumption that anatomical differences both pave the way toward and reflect psychological differences are, for all their curiosity, in the end baseless and ludicrous claims that, if taken seriously, contribute to the still-ongoing oppression of half of the human race, is it not better to take sides with such feminists as de Beauvoir and Freidan and move on without him? Why is Freudianism seen to be valuable for feminism despite these flaws?

Nancy Chodorow has answered this question as well as anyone. In this excerpt from one of her essays, she argues that—within the social sciences, at any rate—only the Freudian perspective can help us understand the manner in which sexual roles are imbedded in us as persons situated in culture. All the problems that Freud has created notwithstanding, she argues, he

> gives us a theory concerning how people—women and men—become gendered and sexed ... how sexual inequality is repro-duced.... In telling us how we come to organize sexuality, gen-der, procreation, parenting, according to psychological patterns, Freud tells us how nature becomes culture and how this culture comes to appear as and to be experienced as "second nature." ... Psychoanalytic theory helps to demonstrate how sexual inequality and the social organization of gender are reproduced. It demon-strates that this reproduction happens in central ways via trans-formations in consciousness in the psyche, and not only via social and cultural institutions. It demonstrates that this reproduction is an unintended product of the structure of the sex-gender system itself—of a family division of labor ... of a culture that assumes and transmits sexual inequality. Freud, or psychoanalysis, tells us how people become heterosexual ... how ... family structure produces in men (and in women, to some extent) a psychology and ideology of male dominance, masculine superiority, and the devaluation of women and things feminine.... Thus, psycho-analysis demonstrates the internal mechanisms of the socio-cultural organization of gender and sexuality and confirms the early feminist argument that the "personal is political." It argues for the rootedness and basic-ness of psychological forms of inequality and oppression.[10]

Chodorow rejects Freud's claims about the relevance of the primal scene as well as his emphasis on the Oedipus complex, but she remains committed to basic psychoanalytic principles. She argues, like Freud, that early events between parents and children are essential to what transpires later in life. In contrast to Freud's nearly exclusive focus on the Oedipal story, however, she focuses on the pre-Oedipal period and on the mother's relationship with daughters and sons. It is in these pre-Oedipal relationships that the patterns we see in boys and girls, men and women, are "reproduced" through the generations.

For Chodorow, the importance of the pre-Oedipal period for understanding the persistence of gender differences is found in the fact that mothering is not merely a biological activity. Although women by virtue of their sex give birth, mothering is a much more complicated activity that is, for all its embeddedness in nature, still a cultural and even political act as well as a biological one.[11] Because "a mother is of the same gender as her daughter and a different gender from her son" (Chodorow 1978, 98), she will experience and treat these children differently. Chodorow emphasizes the difference between gender and sex, a distinction she credits to Freud. Gender is not about biology but rather stands "for the mother's particular psychic structure and relational sense, for her (probable) heterosexuality" and, most important for Chodorow's basic claim that gender differences run deep in the psyche, "for her conscious and unconscious acceptance of the ideology, meanings, and expectations that go into being a gendered member of our society and understanding what gender means."

Feminism has an ally in Freud, Chodorow argues, because a psychoanalytic approach to understanding the asymmetries in mother-child relations in the pre-Oedipal period can illuminate the persistent gender differences we see in adults across a range of cultures and situations. The mother's knowledge, conscious as well as unconscious, that she shares a gender assignment with her daughter will result in a longer and more interconnected pre-Oedipal period for the daughter. In turn, this long and complex pre-Oedipal relationship will create in the daughter a tendency to close affiliation and weak ego boundaries. This is part of what Chodorow means by the "reproduction of mothering." On the other hand, because the mother is aware, again unconsciously as well as consciously, that she does not share gender assignment with the son, she has with him a very different pre-Oedipal relationship in which this boy child finds it easier to move into a stronger pattern of differentiation between self and other. We see again the "reproduction" in a new generation of gender-specific traits, such as a tendency toward dominance.

Chodorow's thesis is contra Freud in that she disagrees with him about virtually all of the particulars. She rejects his emphasis on the Oedipal period and concludes that his views about women are unfortunately based partly on a misogynistic attitude and on "patriarchal distortions" (Chodorow 1978, 141). However, Chodorow defends the basic psychoanalytic formulation that the persistent, robust patterns of gender difference that exist today and have existed in their basic form for many generations are created and then sustained in a dynamic drama of early childhood. Further, while she turns Freud on his head, putting a more positive spin on women's development by talking about affiliative tendencies, and a more negative spin on men's development, by emphasizing the reproduction of dominance rather than any sort of moral superiority, Chodorow's conclusions are classically Freudian in the deep differences they portray between men and women and in the deep and dynamic causes of these differences.

Chodorow has been influential in the specific sense of turning attention to the pre-Oedipal period for an understanding of the development of gender and gender differences, and more generally in supporting the claim that Freud is indispensable for feminism. For example, Carol Gilligan's claim that with regard to moral issues men and women speak in different voices, with men moving within an "ethics of justice" and women within an "ethics of mercy,"[12] depends on Chodorow's formulations about the reproduction of gender roles.

It is perhaps not surprising that both Chodorow and Gilligan have been criticized in some quarters in much the same manner that Freud has been. The criticism is twofold: first, that data from clinical situations compares poorly to the more easily replicable data found in more scientific work; second, that the claims are excessively theory-laden, that the framework in which these phenomena—such as the "reproduction of mothering" or an "ethics of mercy"—are said to be observed also assume the existence of those very phenomena. This last criticism is that the claims of feminists who see depth psychology as indispensable to an analysis of the development of gender differences are, just like those of Freud, circular.[13]

All of which brings us to the issue of *ideology,* which I will define as the assumptions that operate tacitly or unconsciously in an enterprise but nonetheless constrain the kinds of questions that can be asked. The criticisms lodged against Chodorow and Gilligan are made within the particular ideological context of scientific investigation: data from clinical situations are automatically more suspect than those obtained in more controllable situations; the "facts" that arise within a feminist context (and a psychoanalytic one, too) are uncomfortably theory laden. This ideological position holds that it is better to bring a phenomenon out of the clinic and into the laboratory if at all possible. And it holds, too, that facts are, well, more factual if they can stand at least somewhat independently out of a theoretical context.

Feminism represents quite a different ideological context, largely because it considers ideology itself an inescapable factor in the formation of human consciousness. And this is why many contemporary feminist theorists consider Freudianism so central to their tasks: it appears to be the only epistemological framework—within the natural and social sciences, anyway—that allows for the exploration of how the personal, the social, the political, and the ideological interact.

Freud, ironically, would have had little tolerance for such talk about ideology. He proclaimed often that one of the chief merits of science—and he viewed psychoanalysis as fitting firmly within the scientific Weltanschauung—lies precisely in the fact that it can be objective and rational, that is, value free. Contemporary scientific and social scientific approaches to gender, as well as other topics in the human sciences, show a good deal more sophistication than Freud did about the difficulties of untangling fact and value, which is now widely conceded to be a futile enterprise. It remains true, however, that all scientific approaches carry with them core assumptions that function ideologically.

In making this claim about the inevitable place of ideology in scientific endeavor, I am aware that I am asking you to accept something akin to a psychoanalytic premise, that is, about the inevitability of the functioning of unconscious knowledge. The alternative, however, is to accept the narrowly positivistic and scientistic assumption that truth really can be arrived at in a value-free context, an alternative that is today widely rejected, and with good reason.

Within the domain of academic psychology, we can delineate three broad alternatives to the psychoanalytic mode for making sense of gender and sexual difference: the behavioral view, represented by social learning theory; the biological view, represented by sociobiology or its more recent incarnation, evolutionary psychology; and the cognitive-developmental approach.[14]

Social learning theory, which operates within the behavioral tradition, seeks those elements in the environment that reinforce "gender-appropriate" behavior. This approach emphasizes the importance of the child's environment in shaping repertoires of behavior. In contrast to the social learning approach is the biological view represented by sociobiology or evolutionary psychology. In this view, gender-appropriate behavior is a reflection of biological sex; men and women behave, think, and feel in ways that mirror their differing reproductive strategies. The cognitive-developmental approach differs from both of these, viewing children as active agents in their own socialization, "working actively to comprehend their social world."[15]

Arguably, all four of these broad perspectives contribute to our understanding of child development, to understanding how the infant becomes the girl or the boy and eventually the woman or the man. Each of these approaches, however, is also undergirded by ideological, mutually exclusive assumptions about the nature of the most important factors in psychological development.

The core ideological assumption that undergirds social learning theory is that human beings are essentially bundles of rudimentary biological material shaped by multifarious streams of reinforcement or punishment. In this view, the developing human being is not in any substantial way an active agent in his or her own development.[16] Social learning theory also minimizes the very concept of development, assuming that what happens to an individual at an early stage of life is neither more nor less important than what happens later.

With an opposite set of core assumptions, namely that what is most important in understanding human development is the very biological material that the behaviorist would for the most part ignore, and that early development deeply constrains what is possible, the sociobiologist or evolutionary psychologist winds up with a similar portrayal: this time a human being buffeted by evolutionary and genetic forces, no more an active agent than in the behavioral approach.

The ideological position of cognitive-developmental theory is more complex. "Because of the child's need for cognitive consistency, self-categorization as female or male motivates her or him to value that which is seen as similar to the self in terms of gender" (Bem, 229). The child in this approach is assumed to be a more thoroughly active agent than that construed by either the behavioral or the biological approach.

Although in practice these ideological assumptions may not often conflict in the clinic or the lab, they nevertheless lead to quite different portrayals of human nature. The viability of the social learning approach for pointing us toward a true picture of human nature depends on the central ideological claim that the specifics of biology, of developmental history, are of only marginal value. Conversely, the viability of the biological view depends on its ideological claim that human development is deeply constrained by biology—specifically, genetics and evolution—and that the very factors that the behaviorist emphasizes are of minimal importance. Finally, what is noteworthy for our purposes about the ideological underpinning of the cognitive-developmental approach is that while it stresses a developmental process, as does psychoanalysis, the emphasis is on cognitive and non-psychodynamic factors rather than on unconscious ones.

These three approaches, then, offer us the following prospects on gender. By the lights of the social learning approach, it should be possible to identify the sources of, say, gender discrimination and then act to change the patterns of reinforcement to end that discrimination. In this behavioral view, gender difference, gender assignments, and gender discrimination are not found at all deeply in the "mental and emotional bloodstream" and should be thus relatively easy to correct. On the other hand, if our current gender assignments really do reflect, although in a complex and indirect way, an underlying biology whose most important determinants remain evolutionary history and genetic inheritance, then the prospects are quite different. In this view, gender flows quite deeply in us, and role assignments based on sexual difference will prove refractory to modification. Finally, while the cognitive-developmental view takes both the history of the individual and his or her active participation in development seriously, it minimizes the extent to which the person may be motivated by factors that are unconscious in a psychodynamic sense.

Once these alternatives to Freudianism are seen in this way, it is clear why many feminists view Freudianism as an ally in spite of the specific conclusions Freud appeared to draw about the nature and place of women. In direct contrast to the behavioral view, psychoanalysis takes the position that history has consequences, that the patterns that have existed for generations will not be changed by simply altering external circumstances.

And while Freud took a broad evolutionary view as important, indeed essential, for his conclusions, the whole body of his work can be considered to be partly an argument against the view that biology alone, in the sense of somatic and what we today call genetic factors, is sufficient to understand the persistence of psychological traits and patterns. As we saw in chapter 4, Freud was careful to argue that the instincts that constrain psychological life are not just biological but rather exist on the frontier between the bodily and the mental. His claim that psychological complexes are both inherited and freshly acquired as part of the development of each individual in each generation here can be seen as emphasizing the rich and itself constraining interplay between biological nature and personal experience.

Finally, the Freudian ideology contrasts with that undergirding the cognitive-developmental perspective in its emphasis on the importance and nature of unconscious dynamics. While psychoanalysis is, as Chodorow has put it, a "liberatory practice" seeking in a therapeutic context to move a person to the point where he or she can take on a greater sense of responsibility for the future, this is all complicated by the view that the human being is moving in a substantial darkness created by history and conflict. In the Freudian world, change—even liberation—may be possible, but only once the work of bringing long buried unconscious material to the surface has taken place.

It is for these reasons that a rejection of Freudianism would indeed be fatal for at least those varieties of feminism that see oppression and patriarchy as something deeper than can be sustained merely by cultural acquiescence but neither so absolutely ineradicable as the simple argument from a Western and reductionistic biology would suggest.[17]

It appears, then, that a reassessment of Freud's claims about women is in order, given that Freudianism seems, given the options, especially hospitable to the political ends of feminism.

First it should be said that despite his offensive comments about women, Freud's interests in gender differences as distinct from sexuality were theoretical and epistemological rather than political. Furthermore, and in spite of the kind of remarks I highlighted at the beginning of this chapter, Freud saw things in a more complicated and nuanced way:

> [W]e shall, of course, willingly agree that the majority of men are also far behind the masculine ideal and that all human individuals, as a result of their bisexual disposition and of cross-inheritance, combine in themselves both masculine and feminine characteristics, so that pure masculinity and femininity remain constructions of uncertain content. ("Consequences," 258)

Freud cannot be absolved from contributing to traditions of patriarchy and misogyny. It does seem, however, that his interest in sexual difference had significantly to do with the psychology of libido and how his (and to a large extent, still our own) conceptions of masculinity and femininity figure in this psychology. Sexual difference was something of a distraction from the main task of understanding sexuality prior to and independent of gender.[18]

And if feminists—men and women alike—are offended that Freud took such a dim view of women, they should also remember that his view of humankind in general was not noticeably brighter:

> I do not break my head very much about good and evil, but I have
> found very little that is "good" about human beings on the whole.
> In my experience, most of them are trash.[19]

Was Freud's dim view about his fellow human being simply a function
of misanthropy, or was it at least partly dependent on what he thought
he had learned from his work? A related question is to what extent
Freud's more florid and offensive statements specifically about women
mask a more complicated and even useful position, one that, in terms
of specific content as well as ideological assumptions, is consistent
with and sympathetic to the aims of feminism.

The idea that Freud's sentiments about mankind in general flow
from some kind of vague misanthropic attitude does not jibe very well
with what we know about his life. One is on firmer ground in con-
cluding that his pessimism is more intimately related to his psychoanalytic explorations and specifically to his conclusions about the place of
aggression in instinctual life. Despite the fact that aggression is a necessary instinctual factor in the development of culture, both its institu-
tions and its mores, aggression is also responsible for virtually all of
society's problems.

And it is men who are especially implicated in these problems,
for all of the same reasons that women, in Freud's view, are not cen-
trally responsible for the building of culture. This makes men—many
of them moral weaklings, as he says—especially culpable and often
despicable creatures, despicable in the way they torture themselves
with their punishing super-egos, despicable in how they torture others
through the external displays of this aggressive impulse.

If Freud in the end places his hopes in Eros, he also places them
with women, with the feminine. Here we see once again the contradictory Freud, for his disparaging comments about women are undermined
by how they function in the world he portrayed. Returning to the pas-
sages in *Civilization* that opened this chapter, it is true that Freud
describes women as hostile to civilization, as exhibiting retarding and
restraining influences (59). But he does so because he sees them as representing—in a way that men cannot because of their expulsion from

deep relational possibilities by the developmental vector of the super-ego—love, the family, and sexual intimacy. Rather than describing women as retarding and restraining, he might just as accurately have described them as resistive, in some sense the last defense against the demands of civilization. We must remember that Freud is himself deeply ambivalent about the fact that we inexorably develop into a civilized state and are forced to live in this condition. We are discontented—ill at ease, not at home—because of the very processes of repression, renunciation, and sublimation that create civilization. But it is "women who, in the beginning, laid the foundations of civilization by the claims of their love" (59). And as we saw in chapter 6, although the super-ego represents the moral dimension, its punishing aspects, propelled more by the aggressive than the sexual pole of the instincts, are quite worrisome.

In the end, only Eros can save us. But while Freud associated libido with masculinity, Eros is associated in an important way with femininity, at least to the extent that it opposes the work of aggression and the death instinct, and therefore the substantial dark side of the super-ego:

> The pessimistic culture-critic Freud held no enthusiastic brief for the masculine rigours of the triumphalist super-ego. His deep conviction of the superiority of the patriarchal principles of intellectuality and impersonal justice was always tempered by a nagging doubt that it might be women who could best counteract the repressions of civilization, because they are more firmly held by Eros. (Appignanesi and Forrester, 424)

In his paper "Some Psychical Consequences of the Anatomical Distinction Between the Sexes," Freud writes that the super-ego in women "is never so inexorable, so impersonal, so independent of its emotional origins as we require it to be in men" ("Consequences," 257). But given Freud's fundamental ambivalence about the ultimate value of civilization, which of these qualities, even from within his own view, is to be derided? That the super-ego is "never so inexorable"? But we would seem to find a superbly inexorable super-ego only in men who have become "estrange[d] from [their] duties as . . . husband and father" (59). A super-ego that is impersonal and independent of its social origins? If this is the masculine ideal, it spells only trouble; it is "only the weaklings" (61), after all, who gladly or willingly submit to the encroachments on their freedom that civilization represents. But by definition, these weaklings are men, who do not try to restrain, retard, or resist the corrosive forces of civilization in the way that women—by their very Freudian feminine nature!—do intuitively or, to give Freud his due, instinctually.

9

An Anthropology for a
Wiser and Freer Humanity?

"A theory is something nobody believes except the person who made it, while an experiment is something everyone believes except the person who made it."

—attributed to Albert Einstein

"We shall one day recognize in Freud's life-work the cornerstone for the building of a new anthropology ... the future dwelling place of a wiser and freer humanity" (Mann, 427). With the criticism of Freud today more intense than ever, Thomas Mann's homage to Freud may seem quaint if not downright eccentric. Over the last 15 years, critics in fields ranging from basic neuroscience and biological psychiatry to the history and philosophy of science and the traditional humanities have shredded Freud—the man and the work—to pieces. What can Mann have meant, and what relevance might his words have for us today, living among so many voices telling us that Freud is dead?

We have seen in this study that in the Freudian anthropology, we are first of all conflicted creatures, motivated by longing and by a sense of incompleteness. And we are unknowing creatures, fundamentally unaware of what characterizes the drives that propel us forward. The Freudian anthropology also takes history seriously, and at several levels: we are deeply imbedded in the phylogenetic history of our species as well as in the history of our families; at the same time, we have also to deal with the legacy of our personal histories, which are deeply constrained by those broader biological and familial currents.

But we are also implicated in that history. Yes, we are determined by natural and physical laws—overdetermined, in Freudian fact—but we nevertheless have the responsibility to act on our own behalf, to struggle for an enhancement of human freedom, although like Sisyphus we can never completely succeed. And we are imbedded in nature. But although Freud insisted often that we fit fully within the scientific Weltanschauung, the body of his work contradicts this simplistic claim, for the qualities that we possess as human beings, the struggles that we inevitably confront, emerge out of dynamic conflict. The Freudian creature is evolved out of biology but in its engagement with the world is inevitably transforming itself into something that cannot be reduced back to the mere biology that was its starting point.

Having arrived at this last chapter, it will not surprise you that I think the Freudian anthropology is cast off at our own peril. But the question remains, why should anyone believe it? What is the evidence? Where is the consistency, the coherence, the integrity of the argument? Freud's critics make several charges: that his claims cannot be verified; that these claims arise more out of Freud's personal and imaginative life than from dispassionate observation; that his work is not scientific; that in his attempts to further the interests of psychoanalysis, he often behaved unethically; and finally, that in the current moment, part of Freud's legacy is—paradoxically—both a diminished attention to child sexual abuse and a gullibility about the reality of repressed memories.

As it turns out, all but the last of these charges are true. But the way in which they are true must be examined, for in such examination is revealed the anthropology that the critics are offering in place of the Freudian one. First, however, the last charge must be gotten out of the way, since it has little merit or bearing on the question of a Freudian anthropology.

Freud is portrayed by some critics as the progenitor of both a tendency to overlook the sexual abuse of children by adults and the current phenomenon of the so-called "recovery of repressed memories." In the latter case, there is considerable doubt as to whether any such memories exist, despite the fact that in some instances people have been charged with sexual abuse and other crimes, including murder, sometimes several decades after their supposed occurrence.[1]

The basis for the charge that Freud is responsible for a tendency to overlook sexual abuse is his famous "abandonment" of the seduction hypothesis, his early belief that at the bottom of all cases of neurosis lies an instance of actual sexual trauma. Of course it is true that Freud's move away from the seduction hypothesis is a cornerstone of the psychoanalytic enterprise, because it paved the way to understanding the role of unconscious fantasy in psychological life. But to lay responsibility for our denial, underemphasis, and underreporting of childhood sexual abuse at Freud's feet is misguided on several counts.

To characterize Freud's move away from the seduction hypothesis as abandonment is a significant oversimplification. Freud never concluded that all claims of sexual trauma were based on fantasy. Rather, as Paul Robinson has explored, the move was one of emphasis, not anything like a clear-cut disavowal of one hypothesis in favor of another. Further, it is giving even Freud too much credit to argue that his claims about the importance of fantasy could, by themselves, create whole cultural climates in which the minimization of sexual abuse becomes commonplace. The story is more complicated—less reductionistic—than his critics would like to claim. That Freud's ideas have influenced how we look at sexual abuse and how we deal with it no one can doubt, but the claim that Freud is solely or even primarily responsible for this sad and persistent cultural trend is without credibility.

This lack of credibility comes into relief when we examine the role that Freud is also purported to play in the "recovery of repressed memory." In this case, Freud is blamed for those instances in which a person claims to have been abused but in which, presumably, no such abuse has actually occurred. Notice the way in which this accusation is partly a contradiction of the first one. Here, Freud is held responsible not for sexual abuse being ignored but for finding it where it does not actually exist.

It should be noted that these twin accusations are not totally at odds. In both cases, there is a concern that victims have been created because of the emphasis given to imaginative life: in the case of the "abandonment" of the seduction hypothesis, the victims are the children whose actual trauma has been overlooked; in the case of the "recovery of repressed memories," the victims are those who have been wrongly accused.

Once again, however, Freud's critics have oversimplified a complex phenomenon. The cultural trends that help us understand how poorly educated, poorly trained, or unscrupulous therapists could adopt an attitude that says "if you can imagine any reasons why you might have been abused, then you probably were" run deep.[2] In part, this attitude reflects a tendency to want to find sources outside of ourselves for our problems, for our deep sense of malaise; some have called this the psychology of victimization. But ironically, Freud is the figure in our cultural legacy most responsible for showing us that we must look inside ourselves, not for the repressed memories of actual tormentors and tortuous events but for ourselves—for the multiform themes that have become the core of our psychological lives—to understand how we view others. He would have had no tolerance for a psychology of victimization. In Freud's view, we are ourselves ultimately responsible for whatever freedom we manage to find in life; to the extent that we don't find it, we are moral weaklings. He would be as irate at the claims made for recovery of repressed memories as any of his critics, who claim that this trend can be traced to Freud's concept of repression.

That Freud has been so oddly linked with these two phenomena highlights the venom that greets him at many turns. There is something larger at stake here, what Jonathan Lear has called a "war ... over our culture's image of the human soul."[3] This will become clear as we now turn to the other claims of Freud's critics, which, as I have said, are in an interesting sense true, interesting because they also serve to illuminate the agendas and perspectives of the critics themselves.

The criticism that Freud's claims are difficult to verify scientifically is, on balance, accurate. This is not to say that his claims have been falsified. The critics are correct in pointing out, as I discussed in chapter 3, that the claims are often constructed in a way that does not permit such falsification. It is for this reason that Karl Popper ruled psychoanalysis to be outside of science. In addition, when scientists and clinicians have made the effort to operationalize Freud's concepts and test them, the results have been mixed at best. In Fisher and Greenberg's (1977, 1996) extensive reviews of the scientific legitimacy of Freud's claims, many were found to be wanting. While these reviews also point to a fair amount of scientific work that is consistent with some of Freud's concepts, the critics rightly contend, despite Freud's claims that psychoanalysis is a part of the scientific Weltanschauung, that his work cannot be considered science, at least not in the usual sense.

The critics have also pointed to the way in which Freud's claims seem to have grown as much out of his personal and imaginative life as from sober and dispassionate scientific exploration and analysis. Here too they are on solid ground. As I noted in the Chronology, Freud's early life was filled with the kinds of themes and events that might predispose him to seeing Oedipal dynamics just about everywhere. Also, that the cornerstone of his epistemological endeavor was his own self-analysis certainly leads us to agree that a good measure of his data was obtained from his personal musings. After all, the most important dreams Freud dissects in *The Interpretation of Dreams* are his own.

On this point I must indeed go further than Freud's critics, to begin to show how these criticisms ultimately reflect back on the critics themselves as well as on the wider culture that has developed such a complex response to Freud. In an impressive body of work, the historian of science Gerald Holton has made the case that in any scientific endeavor, we can distinguish two different classes of elements.[4] First there are the work and the claims themselves, which belong to what he calls the "empirical domain." This is the actual work of doing science—theory building, experiment, observation, the details that will be found in laboratory notebooks. In addition, however, there are background factors. These "thematic commitments," as Holton refers to them, necessarily figure in the path to the work and the course the work takes. They include the scientist's presuppositions, his intuitive sense of the world, even aesthetic judgments.

For example, if one looks at the work of Newton or Einstein one sees clearly the impact of such thematic commitments. In Newton's case, we know that he was motivated by a conviction that formulating his physical laws—such as the laws of motion—would permit him in some sense to know the "mind of God." Similarly, although Einstein lived in a quite different time than Newton and had quite a different religious sensibility, he brought to his work thematic commitments about the ultimate symmetry and order of the universe; this was one reason he was so aghast at the implications of quantum mechanics, at the very idea that God might "play dice with the universe."

But Freud is a very different case. In pointing to the extent to which his claims rely on his personal and imaginative life, his critics have brought into focus a central way in which Freud's enterprise is different from science as it is usually construed. In the case of Newton and Einstein, although understanding their thematic commitments enriches our appreciation of how they approached their work, we do not need to know anything about these commitments to understand the work itself. This is not true in Freud's case. The personal material—the elements of his imaginative life or his relentless focus on Oedipal themes, for example—is part of the work itself, part of the "empirical domain."

Thus we are able to describe rather concretely another way in which Freud's work departed from science in the usual sense. He made use of autobiographical and imaginative material that, in science as usually considered, is *always* part of the thematic background but *never* part of the empirical domain. Shortly, this will help us understand not only the particular kind of science Freud's enterprise is not but also why the variety of science his critics would put in place of his distinctive epistemological enterprise must fall short of the goal they have at least implicitly set for it. But we must first consider the claims of Freud's critics about his personal and professional ethics, for this too will allow us to follow out certain implications.

The evidence is good that Freud did many things in the course of his professional life that he would have preferred to leave buried, that he overstepped ethical boundaries on many occasions. In his case studies, for example, he rearranged chronologies and overlooked information that would prevent him from making the strongest argument about his already developed hypotheses. In other words, in at least a couple of cases he rearranged the facts to fit his ideas, and then offered his version of the story as support for those ideas.[5] In his tireless work for "the cause," he was not above pressuring clients and their relatives for money. I have undoubtedly left out other ethical transgressions, but the point is made.

So what are we to make of all this? I do not want to cavil about all this evidence, but it seems we are left with two alternatives. We can conclude, for all the reasons just enumerated, that we cannot make use of the Freudian anthropology because, as it has been characterized in the title of one book and in the contents of many others, it is a fraud. Or we can conclude that despite these problems, not only does the Freudian project deserve our attention but also that the very claims of Freud's critics force it on us as a better alternative to the anthropology that they would put in its place.

The route to the latter conclusion, I must admit, seems so simple that it leaves me wondering why the critics cling to their personal attacks with such persistence, expressing a mixture of glee and venom. I think I know what makes these critics so mad, but I wonder that this can be so.

First, let us look at the claims about the lack of scientific merit in Freud's enterprise. As I have said, we can grant these claims. Freud's work was not science in the usual sense, and this may mean that it is not science at all. But if Freud's work is disqualified as science, this may lead us to wonder whether any scientific approach can satisfactorily approach the subject of the self, of the person. As Lear (1990) has suggested, Freud's enterprise leaves us to wonder what a science of subjectivity can be like, and to rethink the very category of science and the kinds and degree of "kinship" between various scientific enterprises.

One may object that although Freud's attempt at a scientific approach failed because his own thematic commitments largely overlapped and replaced the empirical domain, it does not follow that any scientific approach must similarly fail. After all, Freud's critics take aim specifically at Freud, not at a whole class of enterprises. However, these critics claim not to be making attacks ad hominem but rather to be focusing on Freud's methods and procedures. Therefore we are forced to conclude that they are conferring a lesser epistemological status on any venture that so makes use of the personal, the thematic, the imaginative.

Second, let us look at the implications drawn by Freud's critics from his unethical behavior. It was the esteemed scientist Sir Peter Medawar who commented that every scientific paper is a fraud.[6] What he meant is that a report appearing in a scientific journal gives a neatness and shape to the story of discovery that does not actually exist in the process, a process that by nature is chaotic, moved more often by intuitive hunches than by orderly, inductive thinking that follows some sort of Baconian ideal.

And even the wider context of doing science is riven by such factors as personal ambition, envy, and fear (often fear of losing funding). The take-home message of two decades of work in the history and philosophy of science and the sociology of knowledge is that science is a fully human activity, that within it one finds every human foible that one finds outside it. This is not to denigrate science; it is simply to de-idealize it, for it is clear that *pari passu* with the criticisms of Freud's enterprise comes an idealization of science. Anyone who has read James Watson's *The Double Helix,* which describes the very human motives that played an essential role in driving arguably the most important scientific discovery of our time—the structure of DNA— must wonder at the apparent naivete of Freud's critics on this score. Why don't they know better?

The critics will respond, perhaps, that it is not just the ethical questions, not just the lack of empirical validation, not just the way Freud went about insulating his claims from open criticism. Rather, it is the combination of all these factors that forces us to be so persistent in calling for the rejection of the Freudian anthropology. To be sure, Freud brought many of these problems on his own head, in part, as I discussed in chapter 3, by insulating psychoanalysis from the regular avenues of criticism while at the same time so persistently characterizing it as science.

Nevertheless, the question about the epistemological status of Freud's enterprise remains. If it is not science, and neither can it easily be categorized as a form of humanistic learning (though some would and leave it at that), then what are we to make of it? Here, I want to suggest, lie two hidden elements that join Freud's critics together. First, these critical responses tacitly assume that the Freudian enterprise has no epistemological status precisely because it confounds the personal and the imaginative with the empirical. Second, they are bound together by a conviction that the alternative anthropology emanating from the neurosciences and biological psychiatry is and will continue to be more useful than the Freudian one. Let's take these elements in turn.

One way of characterizing artistic activity, including literature, is to say that it contains obvious imaginative and personal elements but in an important way excludes the empirical. If we invoke Holton's framework, in fact, the characterization of artistic activity involves a reversal of the characterization of science. For example, in the case of a novel we find that the equivalent of what would be the empirical domain in science—the heart of the actual enterprise—is actually the imaginative work of the author. The empirical domain, on the other hand, functions for the novelist in the way that thematic commitments function for the scientist: as background—essential background, but background nonetheless. That is, we expect the author of a literary novel to make tacit use of his or her own experience, but do not expect that we can or should find specific clues to the author's actual life experience. Indeed, if these clues are found in extremis, then the work will be faulted as being too autobiographical: to the extent that it remains weighted in the empirical domain, it fails the criterion of imagination. For science, the reverse is the case: while it is illuminating to recognize the personal elements, capacity for wonder, and imagination the scientist brings to the work, the science is rightly faulted if it is light or empty of empirical content.

The essential point is this: no one would suggest that literary works are devoid of epistemological value just because they largely exclude the empirical, instead straightforwardly reflecting their creators' thematic commitments. It seems, then, the very worst that critics can say about Freud's enterprise is that it is something else masquerading as science. But it cannot follow from this claim that whatever it is, it is devoid of epistemological content. However, this is precisely the claim that is made, so we must look elsewhere for its basis, in my view to the conviction of the critics that the neurosciences and biological psychiatry offer a more useful anthropology.

I may seem to have overextended myself by suggesting that Freud's critics grant no epistemological value to the personal and the imaginative. If asked, many if not all of them would surely respond that there is much that they find to be "true" about imaginative literature. But if this is the case, one wonders why they are so bothered by the Freudian enterprise, which, though fundamentally mischaracterized by Freud himself, has so much to do with the imaginative. The reason would appear to be that they are already committed to another anthropology. That is, at bottom much of the vitriolic criticism to which the Freudian anthropology has been subjected stems not from the many ways in which it is and was "improperly" arrived at, but because these critics believe Freud was barking up the wrong tree.

The right tree, in their view, is that planted by neuroscience and biological psychiatry. This anthropology has its own elements and guiding assumptions. Most important, there is a commitment to the idea that mental life is a direct outgrowth of neural life, with the former ultimately reducible to the latter. Notice the very real difference between this way of construing the relationship between the mind and the brain from that offered from within the Freudian anthropology, which portrays the human mind as deeply embedded in a number of factors that have their own developmental vectors—the evolving world, the developing brain, personal experience. Within the Freudian anthropology there is no way of reducing mental life back or down to neural life.

Why should Freud's critics be so attracted to this alternative anthropology? And what is the basis for their conviction?

The first question is, quite honestly, difficult for me to answer. The communities of neuroscience and biological psychiatry have, to be sure, offered powerful methods and technologies for understanding the brain and its relationship to behavior and thought, and to a lesser degree some heuristic structures directed at the same end. The benefits, both practical and conceptual, that these enterprises have given us should not be minimized.[7] But one would think that critics centered in the humanities would entertain the implications of these enterprises and technologies with some skepticism or wariness. After all, once one makes the assumption that mental life is reducible to neural life, it seems harder to accommodate more humanistic claims about the autonomy of the human spirit.

In saying this, I do not mean to oversimplify or caricature the humanities. My point is that while this alternative anthropology does not rule poetic or imaginative conceptions of the human spirit out of bounds, it does relegate them to a distinctly secondary status in epistemological terms. Indeed, from within this alternative anthropology, such poetic and imaginative modes become no more than what Freud in *Civilization* referred to as deflections and substitutive satisfactions. Freud, of course, took such modes of endeavor quite seriously. His comment that psychoanalysis can really only rediscover what the poets have already given us is bolstered by the great use he made of imaginative writers—most notably Goethe and Shakespeare—in developing his ideas.

So even as Freud argued for the primacy of the scientific method, he managed to do so without relegating other modes of inquiry and endeavor to secondary status. As we have seen, Freud was, from our point of view, overly impressed with what a narrowly positivistic enterprise could achieve. But his work contradicted these positivistic stances, as it moved toward a new conception of the human being as at once material—and therefore subject to scientific exploration—and soulful, therefore also elusive of such exploration.[8]

Given that Freud's critics are committed to this alternative anthropology, the second question is about the basis for their commitment. What is it about the claims offered by the neurosciences and biological psychiatry that seem to offer a more useful or more preferable anthropology? On this score, Freud's critics are guilty, in varying degrees depending on the critic, of a naive optimism and a narrow faith in empiricism to the exclusion of other approaches. Almost to a person, they stand outside the actual laboratories in which basic research is done and therefore fail to see the real messiness of it as well as its fatal limitations for offering ultimate frameworks for understanding the dilemmas of living. In a way that would surprise many a working scientist familiar with the inconclusiveness and incompleteness of experiments, their breathless optimism makes it impossible for them to see these limitations.

This is all the more ironic in light of the fact that adherents to the Freudian anthropology are often described by these critics as something akin to religious followers. Certainly these critics are correct in pointing out the shortcomings of an old-guard orthodoxy that still exists in some corners of the psychoanalytic community. It must be said, however, that these critics are themselves in the thrall of the myth of the progress of science; they are paying homage to a priesthood and are thus revealed to have no better understanding of the inner workings and implications of a scientific study than a child observing the consecration of the host at a Catholic mass.[9] They should know better.

Before closing the chapter, I must deal with one issue that has proved vexing for me at various points in this study. I seem to suggest that there is a clear demarcation, an "either/or" choice between the Freudian anthropology and its main competitor in this historical moment. Is this not an oversimplification? In one sense, yes. As Peter Gay has put it, "Freud is inescapable." No amount of Freud-bashing is going to remove from our tools of self-articulation the concepts of repression, of unconscious conflict, of psychosexual desire, and others. And for all that we are, again, enthralled with the newest breakthroughs in the neurosciences, we do not live our lives on a day-to-day basis as if we were really "just" soulless bundles of neurobiological tissue.

At another level, however, something very important is at stake. As I worked on this chapter, the *New York Times,* in a story on the use of antidepressant medication for the young, reported that from 1995 to 1996, new prescriptions for Prozac had increased 47 percent for children ages 13 to 17 and an astounding 298 percent, to 203,000, for children ages 6 to 12.[10] At the same time, it is more and more difficult to receive reimbursement from insurance companies for talk-oriented therapies. I do not intend these statements as a brief for long-term psychoanalytic therapy. Nevertheless, these are worrisome trends, and they are not unconnected to others that increasingly have come to dominate our culture, a culture that is very much as Freud described it in *Civilization:* existentially discontent, not-at-home, ill at ease.

In a penetrating study of the effect of television on our spiritual well-being, Neil Postman has contrasted the Orwellian and the Huxleyan visions of the future.[11] In the Orwellian vision, citizens are prevented from self-exploration through censorship. In the Huxleyan vision, on the other hand, no censorship is necessary since people are kept happily distracted with a number of fixes—"soma," the "feelies." Postman argues that despite our fears of an Orwellian future and its reality in many countries around the world, it is the Huxleyan vision that is coming to pass in America and in those countries that emulate us: as Bruce Springsteen put it, 500 channels but nothing on. We have been druggged senseless by the usually mindless pap that most media present. In this context, the widespread use of antidepressants for the young can be seen as yet another technological agent providing a quick fix that renders much less likely the possibility of self-exploration through reading, conversation, and other means that might render the drugs unnecessary.

I am not suggesting that there is an explicit conspiracy between the media and the drug companies. But we delude ourselves if we think that these technologies do not fundamentally alter the ways in which we live, and consequently, who we are. As Postman put it, "[P]ublic consciousness has not yet assimilated the point that technology is ideology." He allows that we can be excused for being "unprepared for the cultural changes the automobile would bring ... but ... to be unaware that a technology comes equipped with a program for social change, to maintain that technology is neutral, to make the assumption that technology is always a friend to culture is, at this late hour, stupidity plain and simple" (157). Postman's gloss on Huxley, "that in the age of advanced technology, spiritual devastation is more likely to come from an enemy with a smiling face" (155), can seem

both prescient and chilling when one notices recent magazine adver-
tisements for Prozac.[12]

So it turns out that Mann's incantatory appraisal of Freud is in
the end not wide of the mark. The choice is between a view of human
nature in which struggle is an inevitable part of living but in which real
insight and freedom—even liberation—is possible and a view in which
human beings are mere derivatives of biological stuff who can be
steered in certain directions but who cannot really be actors in their
own lives, and in which there is no real call for existential heroism,
only more fine tuning with the latest synaptic fix; between a view of
human nature that offers the *hope* of deep satisfactions and a view that
can offer only an endless stream of distractions; between a view that
takes seriously the possibility that love is a real and palpable force in
the world while also taking into account the darkness and unknowing-
ness in which we as actors move about this world and a view that
refuses to entertain these possibilities unless they can be scientifically
falsified.[13]

Notes and References

Chronology

1. Quoted in Clark, 34.

2. Ibid., 41.

3. Ernest Jones, *The Life and Work of Sigmund Freud,* vol. 1 (New York: Basic Books, 1953), 56.

4. On Freud's naming of his children, see Peter Gay, *Reading Freud: Explorations and Entertainments* (New Haven: Yale University Press, 1990), 54–74.

5. William J. McGrath, "Freud and the Force of History," in Toby Gelfand and John Kerr, eds., *Freud and the History of Psychoanalysis* (Hillsdale, N.J.: Analytic Press, 1992), 80.

6. Barbara Jelavich, *Modern Austria: Empire and Republic, 1815–1986* (Cambridge: Cambridge University Press, 1987), 124.

7. Quoted in Clark, 308.

8. Clark, 401.

9. Carl Schorske, *Fin de Siècle Vienna: Politics and Culture* (New York: Knopf, 1980), 3.

10. Ernst L. Freud, ed., *Letters of Sigmund Freud,* trans. Tania and James Stern (New York: Basic Books, 1960), 344; hereafter cited in text as *Letters.*

11. David Gelernter, *1939: The Lost World of the Fair* (New York: Free Press, 1995), 16.

1. Historical and Intellectual Context

1. Allan Janik and Stephen Toulmin, *Wittgenstein's Vienna* (New York: Simon & Schuster, 1973), 33; hereafter cited in text.

2. Carl Schorske, *Fin de Siècle Vienna: Politics and Culture* (New York: Knopf, 1980), 31.

3. On this broad theme of political liberalism, see McGrath and Schorske . There is no doubt that Freud's life and career were affected by the broad current of anti-Semitism. However, there is considerable debate about the extent to which Freud may have exaggerated its effect on him professionally.

4. Ernest Jones, cited in Norman Lebrecht, *Mahler Remembered* (New York: Norton, 1987), 280.

5. Frederic Morton, *A Nervous Splendor: Vienna, 1888–1889* (Boston: Little, Brown, 1979); Bruno Walter, liner notes for Mahler, *Second Symphony,* Bruno Walter, Columbia Records Y2 30848.

6. Leonard Bernstein, *The Unanswered Question* (Cambridge, Mass.: Harvard University Press), 317.

7. Hilde Spiel, *Vienna's Golden Autumn, 1866–1938* (New York: Weidenfeld and Nicholson, 1987), 134–35; hereafter cited in text.

8. Sigmund Freud, *The Interpretation of Dreams,* vols. 4 and 5 of *The Standard Edition of the Complete Psychological Works of Sigmund Freud,* trans. James Strachey et al. (London: Hogarth Press and the Institute of Psycho-Analysis, 1953–1974); hereafter cited in text as *Interpretation.*

9. Sigmund Freud, *An Autobiographical Study,* vol. 20 of *The Standard Edition,* 8; hereafter cited in text as *AS.*

10. Walter Boehlich, ed., *The Letters of Sigmund Freud to Eduard Silberstein, 1871–1881,* trans. Arnold J. Pomerans (Cambridge, Mass.: Harvard University Press, 1990), 104–5; hereafter cited in text as *Silberstein.*

11. Quoted in Frank J. Sulloway, *Freud, Biologist of the Mind: Beyond the Psychoanalytic Legend* (New York: Basic Books, 1979), 14; hereafter cited in text.

12. J. F. Rychlak, "Freud's Confrontation with the Telic Mind," *Journal of the History of the Behavioral Sciences 17* (1981).

13. Sigmund Freud, *On the History of the Psycho-Analytic Movement* (1914), vol. 14 of *The Standard Edition,* 14; hereafter cited in text as *History.*

2. The Importance of *Civilization and Its Discontents*

1. Peter Gay, in Gay, ed., *The Freud Reader* (New York: Norton, 1989), xiii.

3. Critical Reception: The Abuses and Uses of Freudianism

1. Thomas Mann, *Essays of Three Decades,* trans. H. T. Lowe-Porter (New York: Knopf, 1947), 427; hereafter cited in text.

2. Karl Popper, *Conjectures and Refutations* (New York: Basic Books, 1962).

3. Sigmund Freud, *New Introductory Lectures on Psycho-Analysis* (1933), vol. 22 of *The Standard Edition,* 159; hereafter cited in text as *NIL.*

4. See Seymour Fisher and Roger Greenberg, *The Scientific Credibility of Freud's Theory and Therapy* (New York: Basic Books, 1977); hereafter cited in text.

5. Ernst Mayr, *The Growth of Biological Thought* (Cambridge, Mass.: Harvard University Press, 1982); see chapter 2 for a comparison of laboratory with observational and other scientific methods.

6. Jonathan Lear, *Love and Its Place in Nature: A Philosophical Interpretation of Freudian Psychoanalysis* (New York: Farrar Straus, 1990), 217–18; hereafter cited in text.

7. Frank J. Sulloway, "Reassessing Freud's Case Histories: The Social Construction of Psychoanalysis," in Toby Gelfand and John Kerr, eds., *Freud and the History of Psychoanalysis* (Hillsdale, N.J.: Analytic Press, 1992); hereafter cited in text.

8. Quoted in Norman Keill, ed., *Freud without Hindsight: Reviews of His Work, 1893–1933* (Madison, Conn.: International Universities Press, 1988); hereafter cited in text.

9. Walter Lippman, "Freud and the Layman," *New Republic* (17 April 1915): 9–10.

10. See Terry Eagleton, *Literary Theory: An Introduction* (Minneapolis: University of Minnesota Press, 1983), chapter 5, for an overview of psychoanalytic criticism. Eagleton describes Harold Bloom's *Anxiety of Influence* as an effort to essentially "rewrite literary history in terms of the Oedipal complex" (183).

11. See D. H. Lawrence, *Psychoanalysis and the Unconscious* and *Fantasia of the Unconscious* (New York: Viking, 1960), originally published in 1921 and 1922, respectively.

12. Frederick Crews, a professor of English and a deconverted Freudian, has joined ranks with these critics and, in a series of articles collected in *The Memory Wars: Freud's Legacy in Dispute* (New York: The New York Review of Books, 1995), has often led the charge.

13. Jeffrey Masson, *The Assault on Truth: Freud's Suppression of the Seduction Theory* (New York: Farrar Straus, 1984). The so-called seduction theory was Freud's belief early in his career that behind each neurosis could be found an actual childhood seduction. Freud moved away from this idea beginning in 1897, when he realized that the belief was simply too far fetched because it would mean that the sexual seduction of children by adults was essentially universal. As Paul Robinson has pointed out in *Freud and His Critics* (Berkeley, California: University of California Press, 1993), hereafter cited in text, the story is much more complex than Masson would have us believe. Freud continued to believe that actual seduction took place in some cases but

saw that fantasy was also playing a role in the claims of his patients. This realization paved the way for the development of ideas about the Oedipal complex, the cornerstone of Freud's theory.

14. As an example of this line of thinking, see R. W. McCarley and J. A. Hobson, "The Neurobiological Origins of Psychoanalytic Dream Theory," *American Journal of Psychiatry* 134 (1977): 1211–21.

15. When this manuscript went to press, the exhibit was scheduled to open in the fall of 1998.

16. *Time* (29 November 1993).

4. The Instincts

1. Sigmund Freud, *Beyond the Pleasure Principle* (1920), vol. 18 of *The Standard Edition,* 34; hereafter cited in text as *Beyond.*

2. Raymond E. Fancher, *Psychoanalytic Psychology: The Development of Freud's Thought* (New York: Norton, 1973), 190, italics in original; hereafter cited in text.

3. See chapter 6 for a discussion of Freud's prescriptive views on sexuality.

4. Sigmund Freud, *Introductory Lectures on Psycho-Analysis,* part 3 (1916–1917), vol. 16 in *The Standard Edition,* 311; hereafter cited in text as *Introductory Lectures.*

5. J. Laplanche and J.-B. Pontalis, *The Language of Psycho-Analysis,* trans. Donald Nicholson-Smith (New York: Norton, 1973), 241; hereafter cited in text.

6. Sigmund Freud, *Three Essays on the Theory of Sexuality* (1905), vol. 7 of *The Standard Edition,* 222; hereafter cited in text as *Three Essays.*

7. Sigmund Freud, *The Ego and the Id* (1923), vol. 19 of *The Standard Edition,* 23; hereafter cited in text as *EI.*

8. I am referring to the infant as "he" because Freud for the most part had in mind male sexual development. This slighting of female sexuality is an important issue in coming to terms with Freud, and I discuss it in chapter 8.

9. The theme of separation and loss has reverberated through decades of both basic research in animals and clinical research with human beings. See, for example, Harry F. Harlow, "The Nature of Love," *American Psychologist* 13 (1958): 673–85, and John Bowlby, *Attachment and Loss,* 3 vols. (New York: Basic Books, 1969–1980).

10. For more on this point, see Richard Wollheim, *Sigmund Freud* (New York: Viking, 1971), chapter 4.

11. For further discussion of this translation issue, see Bruno Bettelheim, *Freud and Man's Soul* (New York: Knopf, 1982), 104–5. I disagree with Bettelheim's conclusions about the translators' choice of "vicissitude." In

arguing that "Instincts and Their Vicissitudes" is better translated as "Drives and Their Mutability," Bettelheim seems insufficiently immersed in the English language, and in a way that undermines his own thesis about the humanistic thread in Freud's writing.

12. Sigmund Freud, "Instincts and Their Vicissitudes" (1915), in *The Standard Edition,* vol. 14, 126.

13. See chapter 6 for a fuller discussion of the perverse, the normal, and the healthy.

14. Although I refer several times in this chapter to existential predicaments, I am not suggesting that Freud was an existentialist in any formal sense. As Ernest Becker has pointed out, in his attempt to develop a view of humankind that would allow him to "keep his basic allegiance to physiology ... and reductionist science[,] ... [Freud] seems to have been unable to reach for the really direct existentialist level of explanation" *The Denial of Death* (New York: Free Press, 1973), 98. In spite of this, and despite his own protestations, by the time he penned *Civilization* Freud was clearly exploring existential dilemmas in his own fashion.

15. As I wrote this chapter, a trial of Jack Kevorkian, known as "Dr. Death," was just getting under way. In his opening statement, Kevorkian's attorney made a claim that would be an important part of the defense strategy: that the people who came to Kevorkian for assistance were seeking not death but an end to suffering; death is the route to the goal, not the goal itself. I do not wish to endorse the defense's case, nor am I suggesting that Freud would have, but he certainly would have appreciated the distinction.

I might also point out that in his own death—at the age of 83, after more than 30 operations related to his cancerous jaw, and without a doubt at the natural end of his life—Freud was assisted by his physician, who gives this account:

> While I was sitting by his bedside, Freud took my hand and said to me: "My dear Schur, you certainly remember our first talk. You promised me then not to forsake me when my time comes. Now it's nothing but torture and makes no sense anymore." ... When he was again in agony, I gave him a hypodermic of two centigrams of morphine. He soon felt relief and fell into a peaceful sleep. The expression of pain and suffering was gone. (Max Schur, *Freud: Living and Dying* [New York: International Universities Press], 529).

16. See Gay 1988, 394–95, whom I follow on this point.

17. Erich Fromm, *The Anatomy of Human Destructiveness* (New York: Holt, Rinehart, 1973); hereafter cited in text.

18. E. O. Wilson, *Sociobiology: The New Synthesis* (Cambridge, Mass.: Harvard University Press, 1975), and *On Human Nature* (Cambridge, Mass.: Harvard University Press, 1978); Richard Dawkins, *The Selfish Gene* (New York: Oxford University Press, 1976). More recently, the sociobiological approach has been termed "evolutionary psychology"; see, for example, Robert Wright, *The Moral Animal* (New York: Pantheon, 1994). For a kind of evolutionary psychology that breaks into a territory richer than conventional sociobiology, see Daniel J. Povinelli, "Reconstructing the Evolution of Mind," *American Psychologist* 48 (1993): 493–509.

19. Norman O. Brown, *Life against Death: The Psychoanalytical Meaning of History* (Middletown, Conn.: Wesleyan University Press, 1959), 78; hereafter cited in text.

5. The Unconscious: Dynamic, Conflictual, Transformative

1. Henri F. Ellenberger, *The Discovery of the Unconscious: The History and Evolution of Dynamic Psychiatry* (New York: Basic Books, 1970), 142.

2. J. F. Rychlak, "Freud's Confrontation with the Telic Mind," *Journal of the History of the Behavioral Sciences* 17 1981): 176–83.

3. Sigmund Freud, "Some points for a comparative study of organic and hysterical paralyses" (1893), vol. 1 of *The Standard Edition*, 166; hereafter cited in text as "Comparative Study."

4. This is the first case study in Josef Breuer and Sigmund Freud, *Studies on Hysteria* (1893–1895), vol. 2 of *The Standard Edition*. Anna, whose actual name was Bertha Pappenheim, went on to do important work in the women's movement and in social work. In my summary of the case, I rely on Fancher, Gay (1988), and Breuer.

5. Other authors have referred to the "dynamic model" and the "economic model" on the one hand as roughly equivalent to what Laplanche and Pontalis call the first topography, and to the "structural" or topographical model as roughly equivalent to the second topography. See also Gay : "[I]t is customary to call [the] postwar system the 'structural' system and contrast it with the 'topographic' system of the prewar years. . . . There are many connections and continuities between the two" (1988, 394 n).

6. Sigmund Freud, "The Unconscious" (1915), vol. 14 of *The Standard Edition* 166; my italics.

7. Many take issue with this most basic of Freudian claims, viz. that repression is an inevitable part of the human condition. I deal with this question in chapter 9.

8. Frank Sulloway, *Freud, Biologist of the Mind: Beyond the Psychoanalytic Legend* (New York: Basic Books, 1979); hereafter cited in text.

9. I am indebted for this phrasing to Lear, chapter 6.

10. Sigmund Freud, *Moses and Monotheism* (1939), vol. 23 of *The Standard Edition,* 99–100.

11. See S. J. Gould, *Ontogeny and Phylogeny* (Cambridge, Mass.: Harvard University Press, 1977); hereafter cited in text.

12. Although Freud's commitment to the idea of a phylogenetic inheritance, or ancestral memory, has something in common with Jung's idea of the collective unconscious, both their derivations and their uses are quite different in the two psychologies. While Freud sees the past as reflected in the phylogenetic inheritance as a constraint that strongly predisposes us to rely on past patterns of thought and behavior, Jung's emphasis is on the growth that can come from getting to know the contents—archetypes—of the collective unconscious. In addition, Jung's basic worldview—mystical, with an emphasis on nonmaterial and spiritual reality—is fundamentally different from Freud's, whose bedrock is biological thinking. Jung was not concerned about providing a biological mechanism through which the collective unconscious would be inherited.

6. Ethics and the Place of Reason

1. Ernst L. Freud, ed., *Letters of Sigmund Freud,* trans. Tania and James Stern (New York: Basic Books, 1960), 389–90; hereafter cited in text as *Letters.*

2. Sigmund Freud, *Five Lectures on Psycho-Analysis* (1909), vol. 11 of *The Standard Edition,* 54; hereafter cited in text as *Five Lectures.*

3. See chapter 5.

4. Ernest Wallwork, *Psychoanalysis and Ethics* (New Haven, Conn.: Yale University Press, 1991); hereafter cited in text. I am indebted in this chapter to Wallwork's close and sensitive reading of Freud.

5. Leonard Cohen, *The Future* (New York: Sony Music, 1992), musical recording.

6. These images of good fences, good neighbors, and walls are from Robert Frost's poem "Mending Wall."

7. In this regard, it is interesting to remember Freud's personal comment on the intertwining of friendship and enmity: "My emotional life has always insisted that I should have an intimate friend and a hated enemy. I have always been able to provide myself afresh with both, and it has not infrequently happened that the ideal situation of childhood has been so completely reproduced that friend and enemy have come together in a single individual" (*Interpretation,* 483).

8. See Wallwork, chapter 9, for further discussion of this point.

9. Philip Rieff, *Freud: The Mind of the Moralist* (New York: Anchor, 1961), xxii; hereafter cited in text.

10. In this paragraph, I am simplifying a complex issue in the history of philosophy, mostly because I am unqualified to fully plumb its depths. But two points need to be emphasized.

First, I have borrowed Wallwork's idea of Freud standing "outside the mainstream" of Western philosophy. But Wallwork is speaking specifically here about the question of self-interest. The mainstream, he says, "assume[s] that human beings naturally take care of their own interests and so have to be exhorted to look out for others" (Wallwork, 199). With regard to ethics considered more broadly, Wallwork allows that Freud is not really out of the mainstream but instead pretty firmly embedded "in the Aristotelian-Humean philosophical tradition in assuming that in order to guide action, practical reason must be motivated by some desire, want, or interest" (234).

Second, I have oversimplified Plato's position. While Plato is certainly a progenitor of rationalism and more than skeptical about the material world, his Reason is often erotic in nature.

I am grateful to Kevin McDonnell for guiding me through these issues.

11. Alasdair MacIntyre, *A Short History of Ethics* (New York: Macmillan, 1966), 59; hereafter cited in text.

12. More than once in this study (see chapter 7, for example), I have noted a parallel between Freud's view and the Judeo-Christian worldview, broadly construed. Here, it is interesting to note the connection between the Freudian sense of "not-at-homeness" and the Christian concept of original sin. While Freud railed against religious ideas, there is a case to be made that he was nevertheless embedded in and therefore necessarily influenced by this Judeo-Christian context. (For more on this, see Paul C. Vitz, *Sigmund Freud's Christian Unconscious* [New York: Guilford Press, 1988]). Aristotle, on the other hand—the real pagan!—was thoroughly at home in this world; there was nowhere else to be. I am indebted to Kevin McDonnell for helping me to see this connection.

13. See chapter 5.

14. Lamarckianism, of course, is now discredited. However, two points must be made. First, to be Lamarckian in the years when Freud was building his theory was not unusual. Darwin himself was Lamarckian in believing that habits could be transmitted across generations. Second, although biological evolution does not make use of Lamarckian mechanisms, cultural evolution does. Although Freud seems out of date in clinging to Lamarckianism throughout his life, we can appreciate his stubbornness—it may even seem a bit prescient—when we remember that Freud's theory is not just about biology but also about culture.

15. Richard Rorty, "Freud and Moral Reflection," in Joseph H. Smith and William Kerrigan, eds.), *Pragmatism's Freud: The Moral Disposition*

of Psychoanalysis (Baltimore, Md.: Johns Hopkins University Press, 1986), 10; hereafter cited in text.

16. A good example of this variety of sociobiology is E. O. Wilson, *On Human Nature* (Cambridge, Mass.: Harvard University Press, 1978).

7. The Oceanic Feeling: Freud on Faith and Love

1. Wilfred Cantwell Smith, *Faith and Belief* (Princeton, N.J.: Princeton University Press, 1979).

2. Paul Tillich, *Dynamics of Faith* (New York: Harper, 1956).

3. Sigmund Freud, *The Future of an Illusion* (1927), vol. 21 of *The Standard Edition,* 54; hereafter cited in text as *Future.*

4. Alasdair MacIntyre, "The Debate about God: Victorian Relevance and Contemporary Irrelevance," in Alasdair MacIntyre and Paul Ricouer, *The Religious Significance of Atheism* (New York: Columbia University Press, 1969), 21; hereafter cited in text.

5. For details of Freud's early experience with his nursemaid, Resi Wittek, see Marianne Krüll, *Freud and His Father* (London: Hutchinson, 1987); for how this may bear on his orientation toward religion, see Vitz.

6. See Gillian Beer, *Darwin's Plots: Evolutionary Narrative in Darwin, George Eliot and Nineteenth-Century Fiction* (London: Ark, 1985), for a discussion of the points of contact between Eliot's fiction and evolutionary narratives. I have relied on Gordon Haight, *George Eliot: A Biography* (London: Oxford University Press, 1968), hereafter cited in text, and Jennifer Uglow, *George Eliot* (London: Virago, 1987), for biographical information on Eliot.

7. Gertrude Himmelfarb, *The De-moralization of Society: From Victorian Virtues to Modern Values* (New York: Knopf, 1995). Himmelfarb is here quoting F.W.H. Meyer's famous account of his conversation with Eliot. See Haight, 464.

8. For a discussion of Brentano's influence, see William J. McGrath, *Freud's Discovery of Psychoanalysis: The Politics of Hysteria* (Ithaca, N.Y.: Cornell University Press, 1986), as well as Walter Boelich, ed., *The Letters of Sigmund Freud to Eduard Silberstein, 1871–1881,* trans. Arnold J. Pomerans (Cambridge, Mass.: Harvard University Press, 1990). Peter Gay (1988) also discusses Brentano's influence but oversimplifies the issue of theism.

Some commentators have discussed the curious fact that Freud, so interested in exploring the developmental roots of present-day conflicts and life themes, disclosed so little, at least intentionally, about how he arrived at his negative position vis-à-vis religious belief. Be that as it may, judging from his letters to Silberstein, even as an adolescent Freud seemed to approach the question of the existence of God as much more of an intellectual matter than one having personal, emotional significance.

9. Why was Freud's atheism so confident and painless, while Eliot's was so traumatic? If Freud's commitment to Eros has the kind of religious dimension that I am saying was more routine before liberal theology absorbed his critique, then he is fundamentally unalienated. Of course, part of this may have to do with the fact that Freud was never a theist, which doesn't mean that he wasn't, in MacIntyre's language, a self-conscious atheist; he was.

Eliot, on the other hand, had the theistic and existential rug pulled out from under her. We can say, somewhat anachronistically, that she is one of the people for whom the modern liberal response to Feuerbach, Darwin, and others was made. In the absence of a theistic god, what is the foundation for Eliot's Christian humanism? Basically, a Tillichian ultimate concern for humanity based on Christian principles, not to be minimized but not the old-time religion either. But for Freud's erotic atheism, there is a very firm, and in many ways a religious, foundation. For a discussion of Eliot and humanism, see U. C. Knoepflmacher, *Religious Humanism and the Victorian Novel: George Eliot, Walter Pater, and Samuel Butler* (Princeton, N.J.: Princeton University Press, 1964).

10. That this linkage of love and responsibility operated in Eliot's personal life as well as in her fiction is made clear in Phyllis Rose, *Parallel Lives: Five Victorian Marriages* (New York: Knopf, 1983).

11. Percy was much influenced by Kierkegaard. Becker has discussed the parallels between Kierkegaard's and Freud's depiction of the human condition, and why these two differ so widely on the question of faith.

12. It must be added that Freud's enthusiasm for the scientific Weltanschauung is complicated by his deep ambivalence toward the modern world created by technology. For example: "If there had been no railway to conquer distances, my child would never have left his native town and I should need no telephone to hear his voice" (40). More generally, his distaste for American ways was centered on what he saw as an excessive materialism.

13. Leo Tolstoy, *War and Peace*, trans. Ann Dunnigan (1869; New York: New American Library, 1968), 770–71.

14. George Eliot, *Middlemarch*, (1872; New York: New American Library, 1964), 811; hereafter cited in text.

Freud admired Eliot's work. *Middlemarch* "appealed to him very much, and he found it illuminated important aspects of his relations with Martha. Her *Daniel Deronda* amazed him by its knowledge of Jewish intimate ways" (Ernest Jones, *The Life and Work of Sigmund Freud*, vol. 1 [New York: Basic Books, 1953], 174).

15. This language of loss and disconnection is, strictly speaking, more identified with the school of object-relations theory, which seeks to put more emphasis on the person's attachment to various objects, that is, on object relations, than on pure instinct, as Freud is seen to have done. But without detracting from the work of object-relations theorists, it can be said that

the core of their conceptions is implicit in Freud's own. For more on object-relations theory, see Judith Hughes, *Reshaping the Psychoanalytic Domain* (Berkeley: University of California Press, 1989), and Stephen A. Mitchell, *Relational Concepts in Psychoanalysis* (Cambridge, Mass,: Harvard University Press, 1988).

16. It can be argued that D. H. Lawrence was interested in just such an Eros-ology. See Philip Reiff, *The Triumph of the Therapeutic: Uses of Faith after Freud* (Chicago: University of Chicago Press, 1966), chapter 7.

8. Women, Femininity, and the Import of Ideology

The phrase "import of ideology" in the title of this chapter is taken from Juliet Mitchell, *Psychoanalysis and Feminism* (New York: Vintage Books, 1975), 362.

1. Sigmund Freud, "Some psychical consequences of the anatomical distinction between the sexes" (1925), in *The Standard Edition*, vol. 19, 258; hereafter cited in text as "Consequences."

2. Juliet Mitchell, in *Psychoanalysis and Feminism*, offers a useful summary of all these figures. However, one must also be on guard. As Nancy Chodorow has pointed out in *The Reproduction of Mothering: Psychoanalysis and the Sociology of Gender* (Berkeley: University of California Press, 1978; hereafter cited in text), Mitchell often seems to be an apologist for Freud, zealously defending his most every claim.

3. Hannah Lerman, "From Freud to Feminist Personality Theory: Getting Here from There," in Mary R. Walsh, ed., *The Psychology of Women: Ongoing Debates* (New Haven, Conn.: Yale University Press, 1987), 51; hereafter cited in text.

4. Quoted in Judith K. Gardiner, "Psychoanalysis and Feminism: An American Humanist's View," *Signs, Journal of Women in Culture and Society* 17.2 (1992): 439; hereafter cited in text.

5. The idea of an actual Oedipal complex functioning in psychological life has encountered a good deal of skepticism, partly, but not entirely, justified. In their recent review of the scientific literature, Fisher and Greenberg concluded that some central aspects of Freud's thinking about Oedipal issues are contradicted by scientific studies. In addition, they suggest that "Freud may have exaggerated the degree to which Oedipal transactions are about rivalry, incestuous love, and hate ... [and] underestimated the extent to which positive feelings shape adaptations to the Oedipal phase." However, they also conclude that "the core idea of an Oedipal struggle seems to be sound. The sense of threat to the male child's body integrity growing out of the struggle also looks like a reliable phenomenon. Further, the depiction of the female child's need to master the negative Oedipal position she finds herself in by means of the penis-baby phallicizing process has surprising credibility. But the

potential negative consequences ... attributed by Freud to the Oedipal confrontation seem insufficiently supported; and he is apparently grossly incorrect in his concept of what inspires males to identify with the father and to adopt his values." Seymour Fisher and Roger P. Greenberg, *Freud Scientifically Appraised: Testing the Theories and Therapy* (New York: Wiley, 1996), 276–77.

6. See chapter 6 for a discussion of "normal" sexuality.

7. See chapter 5.

8. Sigmund Freud, *Totem and Taboo* (1913), vol. 13 of *The Standard Edition*; hereafter cited in text as *TT*.

9. But Freud was aware that he was oversimplifying a complex topic: "[T]he contrast between the sexes fades away into one between activity and passivity, in which we *far too readily* identify activity with maleness and passivity with femaleness, a view which is by no means universally confirmed in the animal kingdom" (62, my emphasis).

10. Nancy J. Chodorow, *Feminism and Psychoanalytic Theory* (New Haven, Conn.: Yale University Press, 1989), 176–77.

11. "Historically, the actual physical and biological requirements of childbearing and child care have decreased. But mothering is still performed in the family, and women's mothering role has gained psychological and ideological significance, and has come increasingly to define women's lives" (Chodorow, 4).

12. Carol Gilligan, *In a Different Voice: Psychological Theory and Women's Development* (Cambridge, Mass.: Harvard University Press, 1982).

13. For critiques of Chodorow and Gilligan, see Alice S. Rossi, "On *The Reproduction of Mothering:* A Methodological Debate," and Anne Colby and William Damon, "Listening to a Different Voice," both collected in Walsh.

14. For a discussion of the differences between the social-learning and cognitive-developmental approaches to gender, see Sandra L. Bem, "Gender Schema Theory and Its Implications for Child Development: Raising Gender-Aschematic Children in a Gender-Schematic Society," in Walsh.

15. Lewis and Brooks-Gunn, quoted by Bem in Walsh, 229.

16. Both Bem and Chodorow make this point in their descriptions of behaviorism/social learning theory. Paul Robinson has made the same point in his discussion of Freud's critics.

My point in discussing these approaches is not to denigrate them but to help us understand why a broad current of feminist thinking has been drawn to Freudianism despite all of its apparent shortcomings, especially with respect to gender issues. I must also emphasize that I am talking about the ideological underpinnings of these various approaches rather than how they play out in practice. Practitioners of behavioral approaches do not treat their clients or their experimental subjects as passive objects. And in addition to the concept of reinforcement, behaviorists of whatever stripe—social-learning theorists or cognitive-behavioral therapists, for example—emphasize the observations and the expectations that the person brings to the situation. That being said, it must also be said that the ideological differences remain. While the social-learning theorist or cognitive-behavioral therapist might claim that B. F. Skinner's operational definition of the self as "a repertoire of behavior appropriate to a given set of contingencies" (*Beyond Freedom and Dignity* [New York: Knopf, 1971], 199) is too narrow, he or she would stick to the proposition that these multifarious streams of reinforcement are essential to the construction of the self and would certainly reject the core Freudian assumption of a dynamic and conflict-ridden unconscious as the necessary ingredient in such construction.

17. For more on the ideological underpinnings of biological science and especially reductionism, see Richard Levins and Richard C. Lewontin, *The Dialectical Biologist* (Cambridge, Mass.: Harvard University Press, 1985).

18. On this point, see Lisa Appignanesi and John Forrester, *Freud's Women* (New York: Basic Books, 1992); hereafter cited in text.

Freud's infamous comment to Marie Bonaparte, "*Was will das Weib,*" is often incorrectly translated as "What does *a* woman want?" rather than the correct "What does *woman* want?" The difference is significant; see Peter L. Rudnytsky, letter to the editor, *Times Literary Supplement* (1 July 1994).

19. Heinrich Meng and Ernst L. Freud, eds., *Psychoanalysis and Faith: The Letters of Sigmund Freud and Oskar Pfister,* trans. Eric Mosbacher (New York: Basic Books, 1963), 61.

9. An Anthropology for a Wiser and Freer Humanity?

1. For a discussion of this controversy, see Elizabeth F. Loftus, "The Reality of Repressed Memories," *American Psychologist* 48 (1993): 518–37; hereafter cited in text.

2. "If you think you were abused and your life shows the symptoms, then you were." E. Bass and L. Davis, quoted in Loftus, 525. Loftus refers to Bass and Davis's *Courage to Heal* as the bible of the incest industry.

3. Jonathan Lear, "The Shrink Is In: A Counterblast in the War on Freud," *New Republic* (25 December 1995): 24.

4. A good place to begin an exploration of Holton's work is *Thematic Origins of Scientific Thought: Kepler to Einstein,* rev. ed. (Cambridge, Mass.: Harvard University Press, 1988).

5. Frank J. Sulloway, "Reassessing Freud's Case Histories: The Social Construction of Psychoanalysis," in Toby Gelfand and John Kerr, *Freud and the History of Psychoanalysis* (Hillsdale, N.J.: Analytic Press, 1992).

6. P. B. Medawar, "Is the Scientific Paper a Fraud?," in Medawar, *The Threat and the Glory* (New York: HarperCollins, 1990). This essay was originally published in 1963.

7. Lear (1995) makes the same point.

8. Of course, Freud was not the first person to characterize a human being as both material and soulful; philosophical dualism—with Descartes as its most well-known proponent—makes exactly this claim. But Freud attempted to transcend this very dualism, to bring both body and soul onto the same epistemological ground. In my view, he is an "emergentist/materialist" (see T. Parisi, "Why Freud Failed: Some Implications for Neurophysiology and Sociobiology," *American Psychologist* 42 [1987]: 235–45).

9. For what is in my view a particularly egregious example of this mind-set, see Patricia Churchland, *Neurophilosophy: Toward a Unified Science of the Mind/Brain* (Cambridge, Mass.: MIT Press, 1986). In contrast to my description of Freud as an "emergentist/materialist," Churchland espouses "eliminative materialism," the position that the very concept of mental life will be eliminated by the onward march of the neurosciences, much as the concept of phlogiston left our vocabulary in the seventeenth and eighteenth centuries, to be replaced by oxygen.

10. *New York Times* (10 August 1997).

11. Neil Postman, *Amusing Ourselves to Death: Public Discourse in the Age of Show Business* (New York: Viking Penguin, 1985), hereafter cited in text; see especially chapter 11, "The Huxleyan Warning."

12. See chapter 7, note 12.

13. On this theme, see Andrew Delbanco, *The Death of Satan: How Americans Have Lost Their Sense of Evil* (New York: Farrar Straus, 1995).

Selected Bibliography

Primary Works

All of the following works appear in *The Standard Edition:*

Studies on Hysteria (with Josef Breuer), 1895.

The Interpretation of Dreams, 1900.

The Psychopathology of Everyday Life, 1901.

Jokes and Their Relation to the Unconscious, 1905.

"Fragment of an Analysis of a Case of Hysteria" ("Dora"), 1905.

Three Essays on the Theory of Sexuality, 1905.

"Obsessive Actions and Religious Practices," 1907.

"Analysis of a Phobia in a Five-Year-Old Boy" ("Little Hans"), 1909.

"Notes upon a Case of Obsessional Neurosis" ("The Rat Man"), 1909.

Five Lectures on Psycho-Analysis, 1909.

"Psycho-Analytic Notes on an Autobiographical Account of a Case of Paranoia (Dementia Paranoides)" ("The Case of Schreber"), 1911.

Totem and Taboo, 1913–1914.

On the History of the Psycho-Analytic Movement, 1914.

"On Narcissism: An Introduction," 1914.

"Instincts and Their Vicissitudes," 1915.

"Repression," 1915.

"The Unconscious," 1915.

"Mourning and Melancholia," 1917.

Introductory Lectures on Psycho-Analysis, 1915–1917.

Beyond the Pleasure Principle, 1920.

Group Psychology and the Analysis of the Ego, 1921.

The Ego and the Id, 1923.

An Autobiographical Study, 1925.

Inhibitions, Symptoms and Anxiety, 1926.

The Question of Lay Analysis, 1926.

The Future of an Illusion, 1927.

Civilization and Its Discontents, 1930.

New Introductory Lectures on Psycho-Analysis, 1933.

Analysis Terminable and Interminable, 1937.

Moses and Monotheism, 1939.

Peter Gay, ed. *The Freud Reader.* New York: Norton, 1989. This anthology offers extensive excerpts from *The Standard Edition* and is a good place to begin reading in Freud's body of work.

Correspondence

Freud wrote thousands of letters over the course of his lifetime. Volumes of correspondence with particular individuals are still being published and will continue to be well into the twenty-first century. Here I list a short selection of the available volumes that are deemed especially important or have given me particular pleasure over the years or both.

Walter Boelich, ed. *The Letters of Sigmund Freud to Eduard Silberstein, 1871–1881.* Trans. Arnold J. Pomerans. Cambridge, Mass.: Harvard University Press, 1990. An astounding series of letters, most of which were written when Freud was still a teenager; they foreshadow many of his later ideas.

Ernst L. Freud, ed. *Letters of Sigmund Freud.* Trans. Tania and James Stern. New York: Basic Books, 1960. Includes 102 letters to Martha; the first, written in 1882, opens with the greeting "My precious, most beloved girl," the last, written in 1912, closes with the salutation "Papa."

Jeffrey M. Masson, ed. *The Complete Letters of Sigmund Freud to Wilhelm Fliess, 1887–1904.* Cambridge, Mass.: Harvard University Press, 1985. A very important collection, containing the record of Freud's relationship with Fliess as well as the first formulation of many of his ideas. Freud's "Project for a Scientific Psychology" was a part of the correspondence with Fliess. It is not included in this volume but is found in the first volume of *The Standard Edition.*

William McGuire, ed. *The Freud/Jung Letters: The Correspondence between Sigmund Freud and C. G. Jung.* Trans. Ralph Manheim and R.F.C. Hull. Princeton, N.J.: Princeton University Press, 1974. Like the Fliess correspondence, an important window into the early years of psychoanalysis as well as this central personal and professional relationship.

Secondary Sources

Biography and Reminiscence

Clark, Ronald W. *Freud: The Man and the Cause.* New York: Random House, 1980. Written by a master biographer, with an emphasis on events and relationships.

Donn, Linda. *Freud and Jung: Years of Friendship, Years of Loss.* New York: Collier Books, 1988. An engaging account of this relationship.

Gay, Peter. *Freud: A Life for Our Time.* New York: Norton, 1988. Somewhat hagiographic but particularly valuable for its detailed discussion of the evolution of Freud's thought. Also contains a very useful bibliographical essay.

Jones, Ernest. *The Life and Work of Sigmund Freud.* Three vols. New York: Basic Books, 1953–1957. Written by one of Freud's key disciples and largely superseded by more recent works, but still a source of important historical details.

Schur, Max. *Freud: Living and Dying.* New York: International Universities Press, 1972. Schur was Freud's personal physician from 1928 onward.

Stone, Irving. *The Passions of the Mind.* New York: Doubleday, 1971. A fictional biography, well researched and based closely on historical documents. This is a fun read and an illuminating one, too.

Sulloway, Frank J. *Freud, Biologist of the Mind: Beyond the Psychoanalytic Legend.* New York: Basic Books, 1979. Sulloway has become a leading Freud-basher, but his biography is very important for its exploration of the biological foundations of Freud's thought.

Interpretation and Criticism

Appignanesi, Lisa, and John Forrester. *Freud's Women.* New York: Basic Books, 1992. A discussion of virtually all of the women in Freud's life, interwoven with discussion of his views on femininity.

Bettelheim, Bruno. *Freud and Man's Soul.* New York: Vintage Books, 1984. Bettelheim's argument about the shortcomings of *The Standard Edition.* Overstated, oversimplified, and often simply wrong, this short book is nevertheless a good introduction to issues of translation.

Brown, Norman O. *Life against Death: The Psychoanalytical Meaning of History.* Middletown, Conn.: Wesleyan University Press, 1959. A brilliantly idiosyncratic reading of Freud; includes Brown's often anthologized discussion of Jonathan Swift, "The Excremental Vision."

Crews, Frederick, et. al. *The Memory Wars: Freud's Legacy in Dispute.* New York: New York Review of Books, 1995. Collects Crews's two articles that originally appeared in the *New York Review of Books,* together with responses.

Ellenberger, Henri F. *The Discovery of the Unconscious: The History and Evolution of Dynamic Psychiatry.* New York: Basic Books, 1970. A heroic work of scholarship, Ellenberger's book led the way in breaking the hold of hagiographers and contextualizing Freud and his work.

Fancher, Raymond E. *Psychoanalytic Psychology: The Development of Freud's Thought.* New York: Norton, 1973. A step-by-step re-creation of the principal stages in Freud's theory, interwoven with biographical detail; a very useful introduction.

Fisher, Seymour, and Roger P. Greenberg. *The Scientific Credibility of Freud's Theories and Therapy.* New York: Basic Books, 1977. *Freud Scientifically Reappraised.* New York: John Wiley and Sons, 1996. Both of these books are loaded with information and conclude that while scientific support for many of Freud's claims is lacking, there are a number of areas in which there is a surprisingly respectable amount of such support.

Forrester, John. *Dispatches from the Freud Wars: Psychoanalysis and Its Passions.* Cambridge, Mass.: Harvard University Press, 1997. This collection of essays achieves exactly what its title suggests: a knowledgeable but detached discussion of the issues.

Gay, Peter. *A Godless Jew: Freud, Atheism, and the Making of Psychoanalysis.* New Haven: Yale University Press, 1987. Edifying for the subtle questions about Freud's atheism and its relation to both his contributions and his psychological orientation to the world.

Gelfand, Toby, and John Kerr, eds. *Freud and the History of Psychoanalysis.* Hillsdale, N.J.: The Analytic Press, 1992. A collection of essays by many of the leaders in Freud studies.

Grubrich-Simitis, Ilse. *Back to Freud's Texts: Making Silent Documents Speak.* Trans. Philip Slotkin. New Haven: Yale University Press, 1996. Grubrich-Simitis was for many years intimately involved in the publication of Freud's works in Germany. This is an engrossing book that traces the history of various editions of Freud, looks closely at many available manuscripts, and ends with some suggestions for what a future critical edition of Freud's works should look like.

Grünbaum, Adolf. *The Foundations of Psychoanalysis.* Berkeley: University of California Press, 1984. The most widely discussed philosophical critique of the scientific status of psychoanalysis. A précis, along with commentary, is found in *Behavioral and Brain Sciences* 9 (1986): 217–84.

Holt, Robert R. *Freud Reappraised: A Fresh Look at Psychoanalytic Theory.* New York: Guilford Press, 1989. A detailed reading by a leading Freud scholar, "a concerned friend rather than an attacker or defender."

Selected Bibliography

Janik, Allan, and Stephen Toulmin. *Wittgenstein's Vienna*. New York: Simon & Schuster, 1973. A rich picture of late Habsburg Vienna, and its cultural life.

Kerr, John. *A Most Dangerous Method: The Story of Jung, Freud, and Sabina Spielrein*. New York: Knopf, 1993. An important study of some of the personal factors involved in the institutionalization of psychoanalysis, "an unusually gruesome ghost story, where the ghost who finally devours all the people in the end is not a being but a theory—and a way of listening."

Kitcher, Patricia. *Freud's Dream: A Complete Interdisciplinary Science of Mind*. Cambridge, Mass.: MIT Press, 1992. How an understanding of Freud's work can inform contemporary work in the cognitive sciences.

Krüll, Marianne. *Freud and His Father*. Trans. Arnold J. Pomerans. London: Hutchinson, 1987. A discussion of Freud's "abandonment" of the seduction hypothesis in terms of Freud's relationship with his father. A rich source on Freud's early life and a welcome counterpoint to Masson (1984).

Laplanche, J., and J.-B. Pontalis. *The Language of Psycho-Analysis*. Trans. Donald Nicholson-Smith. New York: Norton, 1973. A dictionary tracing the evolution of Freud's concepts, with lengthy and fully annotated entries; an essential research tool.

Lear, Jonathan. *Love and Its Place in Nature: A Philosophical Interpretation of Psychoanalysis*. New York: Farrar, Strauss and Giroux, 1990. Lear is both an Aristotle scholar and a lay analyst. He brings both lucidity and passion to the development of the claim that love is a force in the world.

———. "The Shrink Is In." *New Republic* (25 December 1995). A "counterblast" in the Freud wars, Lear here argues that "psychoanalysis is crucial for a truly democratic culture to thrive."

Levin, Gerald. *Sigmund Freud*. Boston: G. K. Hall, 1975. Succinct chapters on the case histories, the major theoretical works, and Freud's "theory of literature."

Levy, Donald. *Freud among the Philosophers*. New Haven, Conn.: Yale University Press, 1996. Levy takes issue with a number of Freud's critics in philosophy, from Wittgenstein to Grünbaum.

Mahony, Patrick J. *Freud as a Writer*. New Haven, Conn.: Yale University Press, 1987. Examines the contribution of Freud's literary style to the shape and substance of his theory.

Marcus, Steven. *Freud and the Culture of Psychoanalysis: Studies in the Transition from Victorian Humanism to Modernity*. New York:. Norton, 1984. A thoughtful reading of various aspects of Freud's body of work.

Marcuse, Herbert. *Eros and Civilization: A Philosophical Inquiry into Freud.* New York: Vintage Books, 1955. The most famous reading of Freud to come out of the 1950s, optimistically stressing the possibilities of a non-repressive civilization.

Masson, Jeffrey M. *The Assault on Truth: Freud's Suppression of the Seduction Theory.* New York: Farrar, Strauss and Giroux, 1984. Masson's analysis in oversimplified and self-serving, but this is nevertheless the book that brought the issue of the "abandonment" of the seduction hypothesis to a wide readership. A précis of Masson's argument is found in "Freud and the Seduction Theory," *Atlantic Monthly*(February 1984). Consult Robinson as an antidote.

McCarley, R.W., and J.A. Hobson. "The Neurobiological Origins of Psychoanalytic Dream Theory." *American Journal of Psychiatry* 134 (1977): 1211–21. Useful information despite the rhetorical slant.

McGrath, William J. *Freud's Discovery of Psychoanalysis: The Politics of Hysteria.* Ithaca, N.Y.: Cornell University Press, 1986. A study of how Freud's discoveries were influenced by the political conditions of his day.

Meisel, Perry, ed. *Freud: A Collection of Critical Essays.* Englewood Cliffs, N.J.: Prentice-Hall, 1981. This volume brings together classic as well as more contemporary assessments from the world of literature; includes essays by Leonard Woolf, John Crowe Ransom, Thomas Mann, W.H. Auden, Lionel Trilling, Jacques Derrida, and Harold Bloom.

Morton, Frederick. *A Nervous Splendor: Vienna, 1888–1889.* Boston: Little, Brown, 1979. *Thunder at Twilight: Vienna, 1913–1914.* New York: Scribner, 1989. Two delightful books evoking Freud's city in these crucial years.

Nelson, Benjamin, ed. *Freud and the Twentieth Century.* New York: Meridian Books, 1957. Some very useful entries by intellectuals prominent in the mid-twentieth century.

Neu, Jerome, ed. *The Cambridge Companion to Freud.* Cambridge: Cambridge University Press, 1991. A useful anthology of contemporary responses to Freud.

Ornston, Darius Gray, ed. *Translating Freud.* New Haven, Conn.: Yale University Press, 1992. An important volume focusing on *The Standard Edition;* includes a critical assessment of Bettelheim (1984).

Ricouer, Paul. *Freud and Philosophy: An Essay on Interpretation.* Trans. Denis Savage. New Haven, Conn.: Yale University Press, 1970. Heavy going but an important and sensitive reading placing Freud in the "hermeneutics of suspicion."

Rieff, Philip. *Freud: The Mind of the Moralist.* New York: Anchor Books, 1961. A masterful and influential meditation on all aspects of Freud's work. A wonderful book to dip into for aphoristic bits of wisdom.

Ritvo, Lucille B. *Darwin's Influence on Freud: A Tale of Two Sciences.* New Haven, Conn.: Yale University Press, 1990. An examination of both the general response to Darwin in the German-speaking world and the Darwinian elements in the teachings of Freud's professors.

Roazen, Paul. *Freud and His Followers.* New York: New York University Press, 1984. A good place to begin learning about Freud's inner circle.

Robinson, Paul. *Freud and His Critics.* Berkeley, California: University of California Press, 1993. A thoughtful and, to my mind, devastating commentary on three of Freud's most vocal critics: Frank Sulloway, Jeffrey Masson, and Adolf Grünbaum.

Schorske, Carl E. *Fin de Siècle Vienna: Politics and Culture.* New York: Knopf, 1980. See especially chapter 4, "Politics and Patricide in Freud's *Interpretation of Dreams.*"

Shengold, Leonard. *"The Boy Will Come to Nothing!": Freud's Ego Ideal and Freud as Ego Ideal.* New Haven, Conn.: Yale University Press, 1993. A study of Freud's relationship to some of his role models and colleagues, from Moses to Jung.

Spence, Donald P. *Narrative Truth and Historical Truth: Meaning and Interpretation in Psychoanalysis.* New York: Norton, 1982. An important discussion about philosophical assumptions underlying the therapeutic process.

Stepansky, Paul E., ed. *Freud, Appraisals and Reappraisals: Contributions to Freud Studies.* 3 vols. Hillsdale, N.J.: Analytic Press, 1986–1988. A wide-ranging collection.

Wallwork, Ernest. *Psychoanalysis and Ethics.* New Haven, Conn.: Yale University Press, 1991. A close, sensitive, and insightful reading of Freud.

Whyte, Lancelot Law. *The Unconscious before Freud.* New York: Anchor Books, 1962. "A study of the idea of the unconscious over the two hundred years before Freud."

Wittels, Fritz. *Freud and His Time.* New York: Grosset and Dunlap, 1931. As John Kerr has pointed out, this work is still of value in part because it predates the institutionalizing work of the Jones biography.

Zaretsky, Eli. "Freud's Hatchet Man in an Age of Deidealization." *American Imago* 53.4 (1996): 385–403. A response to Frederick Crews.

Index

abreaction, 48

academic psychology, 105

acquired characteristics, inheritance of, 55

Adam Bede (Eliot), 78

aggression, 34; benign, 41; and civilization, 109; environmentalist approach to, 39; and Eros, 65, 66–67, 110; in geopolitics, 41–42; instinctivist approach to, 40; malignant, 41; and super-ego, 68, 70, 71

alienation, postmodern, 79

anal stage, 32

ancestral memory, 98, 133n. 12. *See also* phylogeny

Andreas-Salomé, Lou, Freud's letter to, 58–59

anesthesia, 46–47

animals, humans differences from, 54

Anna O., 10, 47–48, 132n. 18

anthropology. *See* Freudian anthropology

antidepressants, 123, 124, 125

anti-Semitism, 4, 81, 128n. 3

anxiety dreams, 35

Anxiety of Influence (Bloom), 129n. 10

Aristotle, 134n. 12; and ethics, 74–75; *Nichomachean Ethics,* 74

arrested development, 62

art, 88, 120–21, 122

Assault on Truth: Freud's Suppression of the Seduction Theory, The (Masson), 129–30n. 13

atheism, 79, 80, 86, 136n. 9

Auden, W. H., "In Memory of Sigmund Freud," 15

Austria, annexation of, 3, 11. *See also* Vienna

Austria-Hungary, war with Prussia, 4

Balkan nations, 4

Bass, E., *Courage to Heal,* 139n. 2

Becker, Ernest, 136n. 11; *The Denial of Death,* 131n. 14

Index

Cohen, Leonard, 66
collective unconscious, 133n. 12
compromise formations, 51, 70
compulsion to repeat, 36–37, 38
conflictual unconscious, 45–52. *See also* unconscious
conscience, 67–68, 77
constancy, principle of, 28
Copernicus, Nicolaus, 16, 19
cosmology, 17
cosmos, 88, 89. *See also* faith; religion
Courage to Heal (Bass and Davis), 139n. 2
Crews, Frederick, *The Memory Years: Freud's Legacy in Dispute,* 129n. 12
cross-inheritance, 99
cruelty, 42, 43

Darwin, Charles: contemporary views of, 19; impact of, 16; influence on Freud, 9, 75; and Lamarckianism, 134n. 14; *Origin of Species, The,* 86; and primal horde, 55
Darwinian evolutionary theory: and aggression, 40; Freud's interest in, 7, 85–86; influence on Eliot, 85–86; and Lamarckianism, 75
Das Leben Jesu (Strauss), 86
Davis, L., *Courage to Heal,* 139n. 2
Dawkins, Richard, 40
death, 13, 131n. 15. *See also* death instinct
death instinct, 4, 6, 33–43; in animals, 54; Catlin on, 19; purpose of, 27, 28, 76; and superego, 70, 71, 110. *See also* instincts
de Beauvoir, Simone, 95; *Second Sex,* 21
defense mechanisms, 49, 51. *See also* repression

Denial of Death, The (Becker), 131n. 14
Descartes, René, 28–29, 140n. 8
development theory. *See* Darwin, Charles; Darwinian evolutionary theory; Lamarck, Jean-Baptiste de Monet de; Lamarckianism
differentiation, 52
disconnection, 136–37n. 15
Double Helix, The (Watson), 119
dreams: anxiety, 35; and Mahler's Third Symphony, 5; of soldiers with traumatic neuroses, 35–36
drive. *See* instincts
dualism, 13, 38, 140n. 8
Dubliners (Joyce), 22
Duffus, R. L., 19
dynamic model, 132n. 5
dynamic unconscious, 35, 45–52. *See also* unconscious

Eagleton, Terry, *Literary Theory: An Introduction,* 129n. 10
economic model, 132n. 5
ego: in animals, 54; and id, 76, 83–84; overview of, 49, 51, 52; role of, 69, 71; and superego, 67, 68, 70
ego instincts, 37
Einstein, Albert, 112, 117
eliminative materialism, 140n. 9
Eliot, George, 85, 92, 136n. 9; *Adam Bede,* 78; intellectual development of, 86–87; *Middlemarch,* 86, 90, 136n. 14; and Percy, 88; and redemption, 89
emergentist/materialist, Freud as, 140n. 9
empirical domain, 116, 117, 119, 120–21
Enlightenment, 81

151

Index

Index

reinforcement, 138–39n. 16
relationships, 34
religion, 78–92, 134n. 12, 135n. 8, 136n. 9. *See also* faith
remorse. *See* guilt
repetition compulsion, 36–37, 38
repressed memories, 113. *See also* recovered memory syndrome
repression, 50, 52, 61, 71, 132n. 7
reproduction, 29, 31, 60, 61
Reproduction of Mothering, The (Chodorow), 137n. 2
Resurrection (Mahler's Second Symphony), 5
Richards, Keith, 43
Ricouer, Paul, *Freud and Philosophy*, 21
Ringstrasse, 3, 4
Robinson, Paul, 114; *Freud and His Critics*, 129–30n. 13
Rolland, Romaine, 80, 82, 85, 91; Freud's letter to, 64
Rome, archaeology of, Freud's metaphor of, 50, 51
Rorty, Richard, 76–77

sacred, 80
Salpêtrière clinic, 9
Sarajevo, assassination of Ferdinand in, 4
Schnitzler, Arthur, 5–6
Schoenberg, Arnold, 5
Schorske, Carl, on Vienna, 5
Schur, Max, *Freud: Living and Dying*, 131n. 15
science: history and philosophy of, attack on Freudian anthropology, 23; ideology in, 104–5; and religion, 81, 87; and transcendence, 88
scientific method, Freud's, 16–18, 118–20, 123
scientific Weltanschauung, 8, 16, 88, 136n. 12

Second Sex (de Beauvoir), 21
"second wave" of feminism, 95
seduction hypothesis, 23, 114, 115, 129–30n. 13
self: behaviorists' definition of, 138–39n. 16; natural history of, 91 (*see also* phylogeny)
self-categorization, 106
self-exploration, Viennese roots of, 5
self-love, 37–38
self-preservative instincts, 31, 37
separation, 130n. 9
sex instinct, 27, 28–33; in animals, 54; and ethics, 60–64; transformation of, 42. *See also* Eros; instincts; love
sexual abuse, of children. *See* child sexual abuse
sexual conflict, and neurosis, 9, 10. *See also* Sex instinct
sexuality, 100. *See also* Sex instinct
Sexual Politics (Millet), 21
Shakespeare, William, 7, 21, 33, 122
Silberstein, Freud's letters to, 135n. 8
Sisyphus, 113
Skinner, B. F., 39, 138–39n. 16
Smith, William Cantwell, 79
social learning theory, 105, 106–7, 138–39n. 16
sociobiology, 40, 106, 132n. 18
soldiers, with traumatic neuroses, 35–36
"Some Psychical Consequences of the Anatomical Distinction Between the Sexes" (Freud), 110
Sons and Lovers (Lawrence), 22
Spencer, Herbert, 86
Strachey, John, review of *Civilization and Its Discontents*, 19
Strauss, George Friedrich, *Das Leben Jesu*, 86
Studies in Hysteria (Freud and Breuer), 10, 132n. 18

The Author

Thomas Parisi, a native of Brooklyn, New York, teaches at Saint Mary's College in Notre Dame, Indiana, where he is currently chair of the psychology department. He received his Ph.D. in biopsychology from the University of Rochester in 1980. His interest in Freud was sparked when, as a graduate student and postdoctoral laboratory researcher, he realized that an understanding of Freud's journey could be helpful in thinking about neuroscientific reductionism in our day. In addition to his work on Freud, which has appeared in *American Psychologist, Philosophy and Biology,* and other journals, he has published scientific papers on topics ranging from autoshaping in the pigeon to the neurophysiology of the startle reflex in the developing rat. He teaches a range of courses at the intersection of biology and psychology as well as a seminar on historical and philosophical dimensions of psychology. He also teaches interdisciplinary core courses with colleagues in literature, philosophy, biology, and humanistic studies. This is his first book.

The Editor

Robert Lecker is professor of English at McGill University in Montreal. He received his Ph.D. from York University. Professor Lecker is the author of numerous critical studies, including *On the Line* (1982), *Robert Kroetch* (1986), *An Other I* (1988), and *Making It Real: The Canonization of English-Canadian Literature* (1995). He is the editor of the critical journal *Essays on Canadian Writing* and of many collections of critical essays, the most recent of which is *Canadian Canons: Essays in Literary Value* (1991). He is the founding and current general editor of Twayne's Masterwork Studies and the editor of the Twayne World Authors Series on Canadian writers. He is also the general editor of G. K. Hall's Critical Essays on World Literature series.